Engineering Chemistry Laboratory Manual

Applicable for all B.E./B.Tech Branch

Department of Applied sciences

AUTHOR: Dr. Vineeta Kumari

Assistant Professor

Jharkhand Rai University

Raja Ulatu , Ranchi- 834005

Published by **SPI Publications**, www.spipublications.in

SPI, the **SPI logo**, and **Split Poetry India** are trademarks of **SPI Publications**, or its affiliates.

ISBN-13: 978-93-49860-87-2

First Edition 2025

SPI Publications

Corporate & Editorial Office
117/2, Sector 37, Khandsa Road,
Gurgaon, Haryana 122 001
Phone: +91 98355 52940
Email: contact@spipublications.in
Website: www.spipublications.in

Processed and Printed in India

GENERAL GUIDELINES AND SAFETY INSTRUCTIONS

1. Log your entry immediately upon entering the laboratory and adhere strictly to your assigned lab schedule.

2. Follow all instructions—both written and spoken—given by the teacher or lab instructor. If anything is unclear, consult them without hesitation.

3. Never work in the lab by yourself. Always be accompanied by a lab partner or an instructor/teaching assistant.

4. Wearing the prescribed uniform and displaying your ID card is compulsory during lab sessions.

5. Avoid loose clothing or jewelry in the lab, as items like rings and necklaces can conduct electricity.

6. Mobile phones must be turned off in the lab. Bags should be stored in the designated rack.

7. Maintain cleanliness in the lab at all times. Eating or drinking inside the lab is strictly prohibited.

8. Any form of deliberate misconduct will result in being barred from the laboratory.

9. Do not use any lab equipment without first reading the associated safety guidelines. Always review the lab manual and experiment procedures beforehand.

10. Complete all circuit connections and ensure proper setup before turning on the power. Never adjust or rewire a circuit while it is powered.

11. Avoid direct contact with live electrical circuits to prevent accidents.

12. Do not force connectors into sockets; insert them gently and correctly.

13. Never attempt to experiment using power directly from the wall outlet.

14. Immediately notify the lab instructor/teacher if you encounter any hazardous or abnormal situations such as malfunctioning equipment, damaged wires, or burning smells. If unsure, activate the emergency shutdown.

15. Refrain from using any damaged tools, wires, or connectors. Report and return such items to the instructor.

16. Know the location of fire extinguishers and first aid kits within the laboratory.

17. After finishing your experiment, return all lab equipment—including breadboards, trainer kits, wires, and CRO probes—to the staff. Do not remove any items from the lab without authorization.

18. Always bring your observation book and lab record to each session. Enter current readings in the observation book, and ensure previous experiments are documented in the lab record. Both should be reviewed and signed by the faculty during each lab.

PREFACE

This "Engineering Chemistry Laboratory Manual" is designed for first-semester B.E/B. Tech students across all branches, aligning fully with the AICTE/UGC syllabus under the Outcome-Based Education Credit System.

The manual systematically presents a range of qualitative, quantitative, Instrumental and physical chemistry experiments in a clear and accessible manner.

It is intended to serve as a practical resource for both students and instructors.

Feedback and suggestions for improving the manual are most welcome and will be sincerely appreciated.

Readers are encouraged to share their insights and recommendations for the enhancement of this book.

Dr. Vineeta Kumari

INDEX

Experiment-1

Know your Lab

Laboratory Apparatus

Laboratory equipment. Laboratory equipment encompasses a variety of tools and instruments designed to perform specific functions within a lab setting. These devices are utilized by scientists, educators, students, and healthcare professionals. Common uses of laboratory equipment include weighing substances, preparing and mixing chemical solutions, and cleaning laboratory glassware.

Microscope:

A microscope is a widely used laboratory tool that enables the observation of objects too small to be seen unaided. Light microscopes function by illuminating the specimen and magnifying it through a series of lenses, while electron microscopes use a beam of electrons to achieve much higher magnification levels.

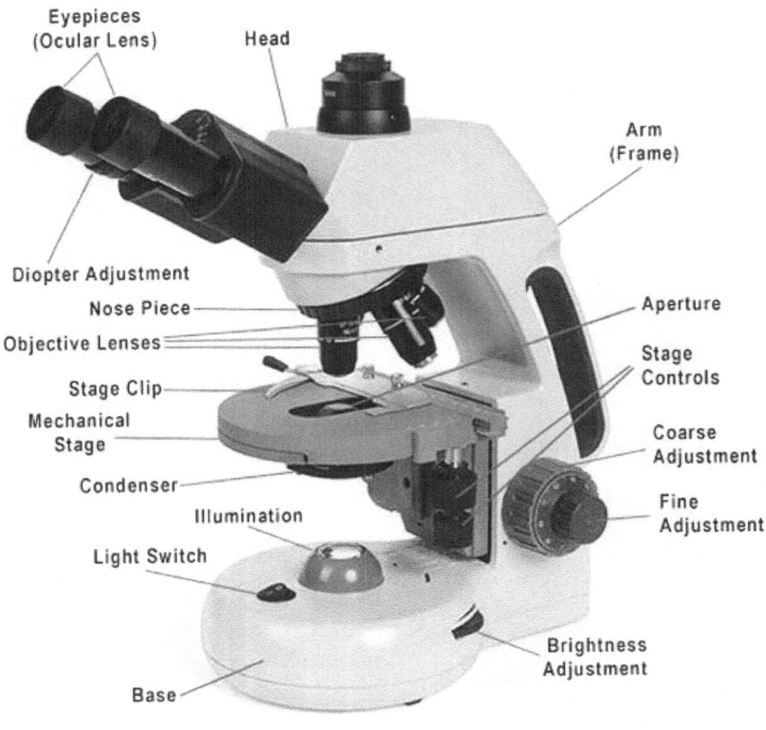

Test Tube:

A test tube is a laboratory container commonly used for holding and mixing liquid chemicals. It is cylindrical in shape, resembling a finger, with one open end. Test tubes come in various sizes, with the standard size typically being 18 x 150 mm.

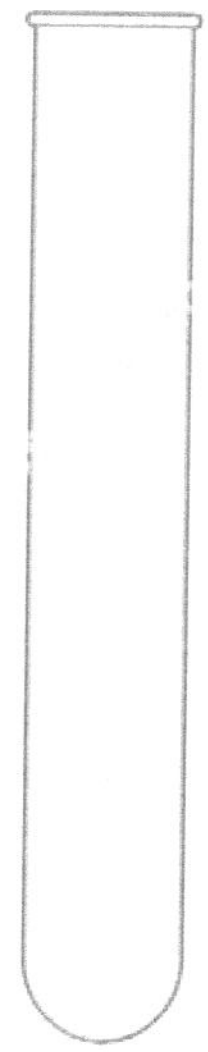

Watch glass:

A watch glass is a frequently used laboratory tool made of concave glass. It is typically used for holding solid substances, evaporating liquids, and gently heating small quantities of materials.

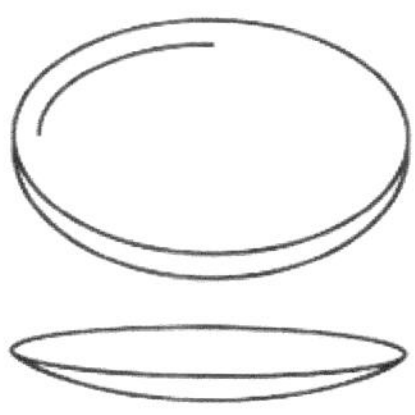

Crucible:

A crucible is a small vessel typically made from porcelain. Unlike some types of laboratory glassware that can crack or break when heated, the crucible is designed to withstand high temperatures. It usually comes with a lid to help contain smoke or vapors during heating.

Volumetric Flasks:

Volumetric flasks are commonly used pieces of equipment in chemistry laboratories. They are specially calibrated glass containers designed to hold precise volumes of liquid at specific temperatures. These flasks are primarily used to prepare standard solutions and perform accurate dilutions. Available in various capacities, volumetric flasks typically come in sizes such as 50 ml, 125 ml, 250 ml, 500 ml, and 1000 ml, depending on the required volume of solution.

Beakers:

Similar to test tubes, beakers are used to heat, mix, and store different types of materials. Beakers are cylindrical containers without rounded bottoms and have a spout and a flat base. They are also available in several sizes

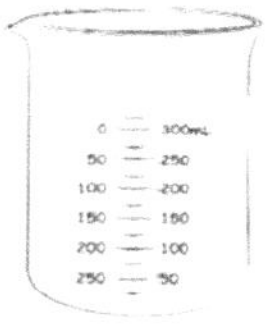

Bunsen burner:

This device is used for sterilizing and heating things. Natural gas or liquefied petroleum gas, such as methane, could be utilized.

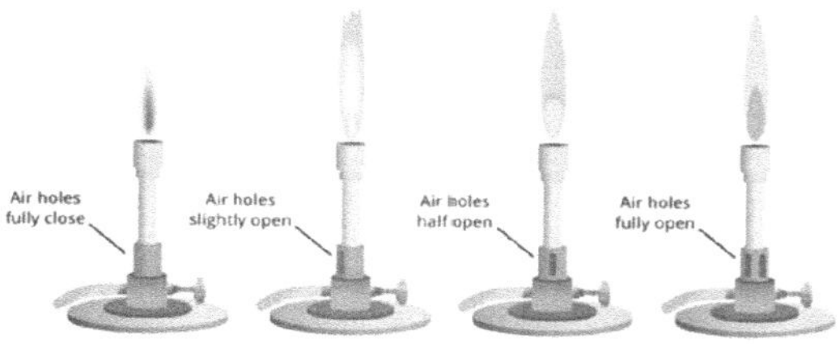

Spatula:

A laboratory spatula is similar to a kitchen spatula, except it is considerably smaller. Spatulas are tiny, hand-held instruments for scooping and transferring solids. They can also be used to apply paste-like treatments. Most spatulas are used with various chemicals, typically resistant to heat and acid.

Magnifying Glass:

This specific piece of lab equipment creates a magnified image of an object. It is a convex lens covered with a handle-equipped frame.

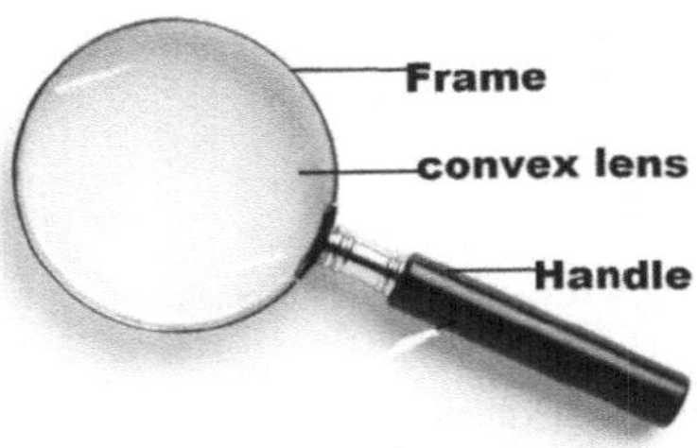

Spring Balance:

A spring balance is also known as a newton meter. The tension of a spring on the scale is used to calculate the object's weight. On one side, there is a spring, and on the other, there is a hook.

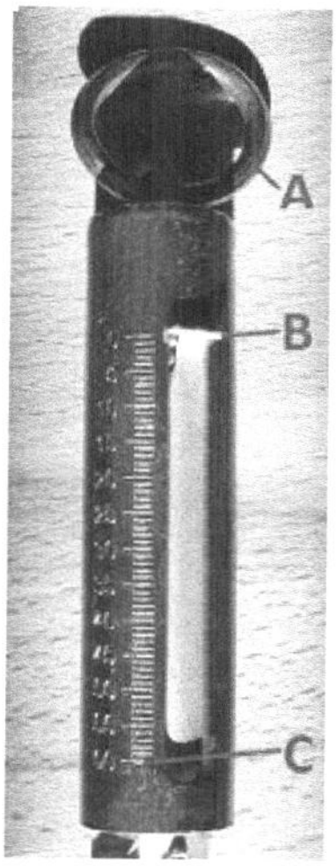

Dropper:

A dropper is also known as a Pasteur pipette. It is a small glass or plastic pipe with a rubber tip on one end. Its purpose is to give little volumes of liquids one drop at a time.

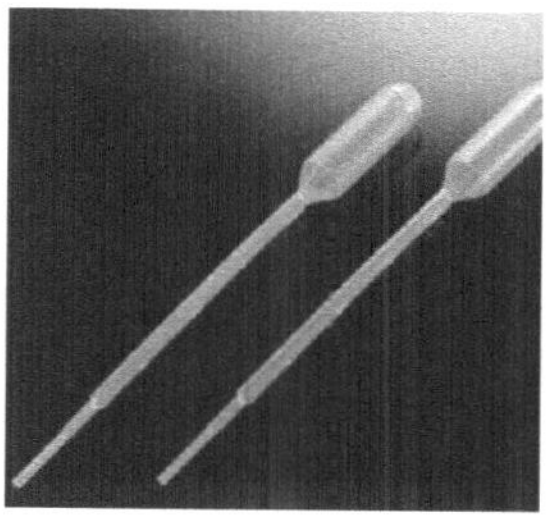

Measuring Cylinder:

This typical laboratory instrument is used to determine the volume of a liquid. It is calibrated, with each marker indicating the quantity of chemical used. This glassware is cylindrical and narrow, as the name indicates.

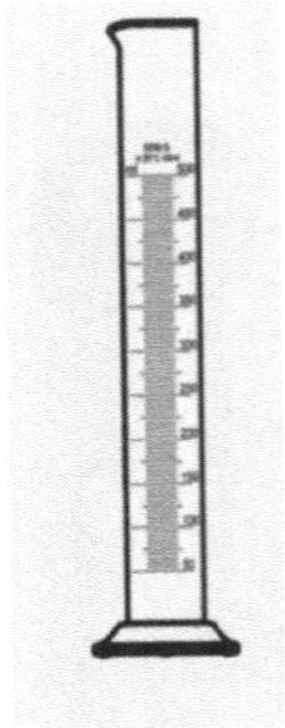

Thermometer:

We all have used thermometers at home, so we are all familiar with them. Laboratory thermometers are almost identical in that they measure the temperature of substances (instead of body temperature) and have a high level of accuracy.

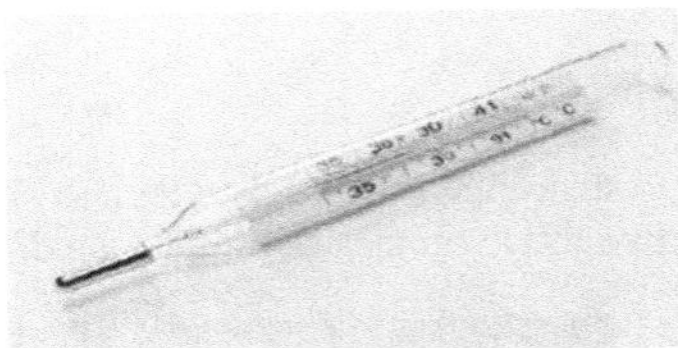

Burette:

A basic piece of chemical laboratory equipment used to dispense volumes of material. It is often used in titrations. The stopcock is located at the bottom of the long-graded tube. The burettes are 50ml, 25ml, and 10ml.

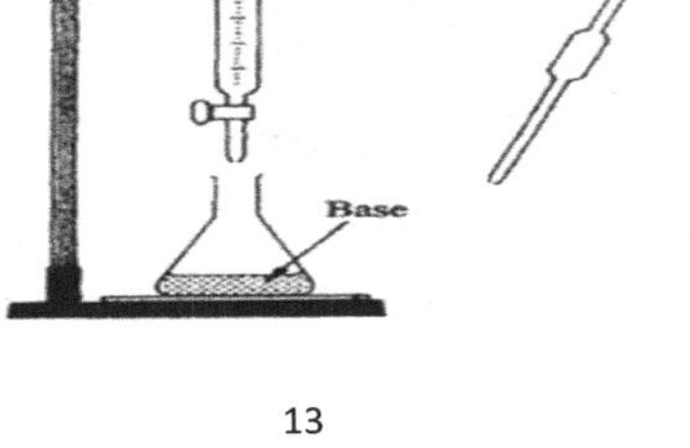

Balance:

Because certain experiments demand correct quantities of ingredients, solids are often weighed before use. A balance is a device that is used to consider materials. The most popular balance types are analytical and top loading balances.

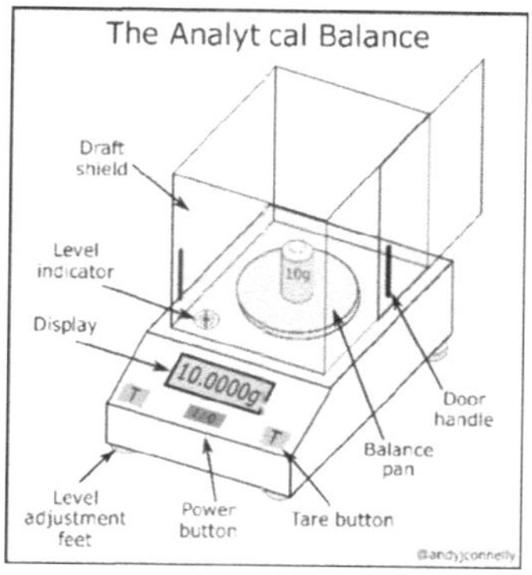

Funnels:

Funnels are another essential kind of device. They are used to transfer chemicals into small-mouthed receptacles. Filter, thistle, and falling funnels are some of the various types, and each has a specific purpose. Buchner and Hirsch s funnels are excellent examples of organic chemistry laboratory gear.

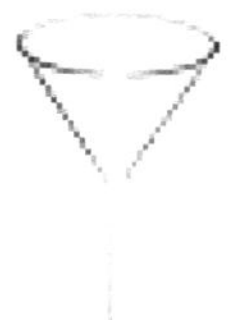

Wash Bottle:

A wash bottle is a squeeze container used to clean and rinse glassware. The majority of wash bottles are plastic. Depending on the task, you may fill it with ethanol or deionized water.

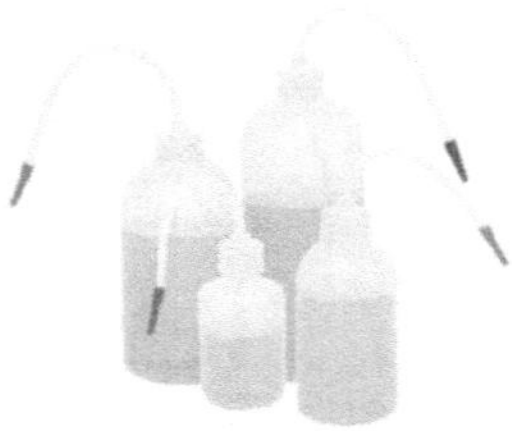

Tongs:

You are often exposed to chemicals, heat, and other potentially harmful substances when working in a laboratory. Tongs are used to grab dangerous things and handle hot containers. Each sort of tong is intended for a particular purpose. Beaker, utility, and crucible tongs are common examples.

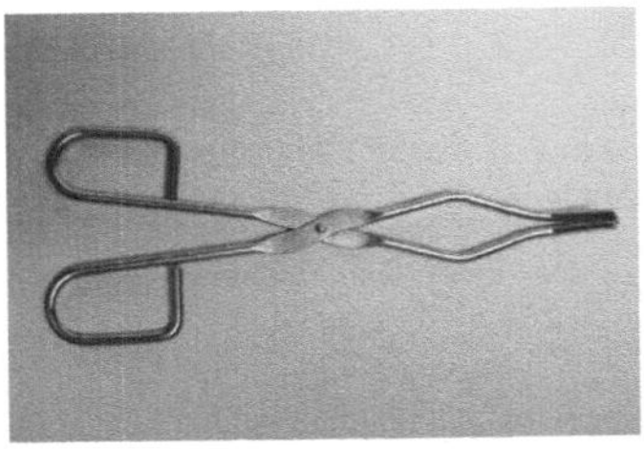

Ammeter:

This is a piece of equipment that is present in every physics lab. An ammeter is a tool to gauge how much electricity moves across a circuit.

Brushes for Test Tubes:

Without a cleaning tool, our laboratory equipment list would be incomplete. Test tubes, flasks, and beakers are cleaned using cleaning brushes. After usage, all equipment should be cleaned and safely stored.

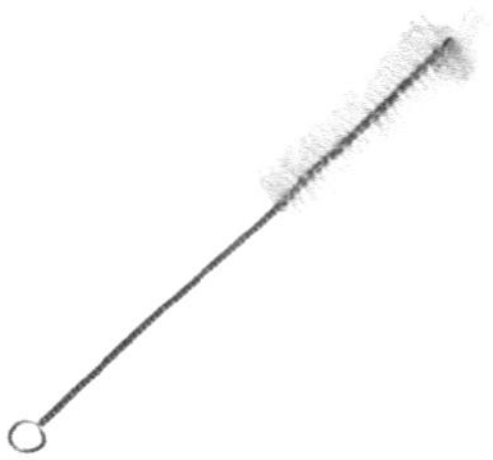

Experiment-2

Determine the Strength of NaOH Solution (Standard Hydrochloric acid Solution Supplied).

Theory of experiment: Titration is a common analytical method used to calculate the concentration of an unknown solution. In this process, a reagent of known concentration and volume (called the titrant) is gradually added to a solution of unknown concentration (the analyte) until the chemical reaction between the two is complete. An appropriate indicator is used to signal the end point of the reaction, typically through a color change.

Acid-Base Titration:

A widely used form of titration involves the neutralization of an acid by a base. This reaction results in the formation of salt and water. For instance, one mole of hydrochloric acid (HCl) reacts completely with one mole of sodium hydroxide (NaOH) to form sodium chloride (NaCl) and water (H_2O):

$$HCl + NaOH \rightarrow NaCl + H_2O$$

(Acid) + (Base) → (Salt) + (Water)

Molarity: The concentration of a solution can be expressed in several ways; however, molarity (M) is the most commonly used unit. It is defined as the number of moles of solute present in one liter of solution

Molarity (M) = Moles of solute / Volume of solution in liters

Apparatus required:

Burette

Pipette

Conical flasks (4)

Beaker

Funnel

Stand and clamp

Pipette filler

Measuring cylinder

Dropper

Safety goggles

Chemicals Required:

Hydrochloric acid (HCl), 0.09756 $mol \cdot dm^{-3}$ (standard solution)

Sodium hydroxide (NaOH), concentration unknown

Phenolphthalein indicator

Procedure:

1. Measure 10 mL of the hydrochloric acid solution using a pipette and transfer it into a conical flask.

2. Add 2 to 3 drops of phenolphthalein indicator to the acid.

3. Fill the burette with sodium hydroxide solution up to just below the 0.00 mL mark. Before starting, rinse the burette twice with \~5 mL of the NaOH solution to avoid contamination.

4. Make sure no air bubbles are trapped in the burette tip by letting a few drops pass through the stopcock.

5. Position the conical flask beneath the burette and slowly add the sodium hydroxide solution while continuously swirling the flask.

6. As the pink color begins to appear, reduce the flow to one drop at a time. The end point is reached when a faint pink shade remains visible for at least 30 seconds.

7. Record the final volume of NaOH added from the burette.

8. Discard the titrated solution and rinse the conical flask.

9. Repeat the procedure to perform at least three titrations, continuing until you obtain three consistent (concordant) readings that vary by no more than 1.0%.

Observations:

No of observation	Volume of NaOH solution in mL	Burette reading Initial Final	Different	Constant	Indicator used
Trial-1					
Trial-2					
Trial-3					

Calculations:

V_1=Volume of HCl

N_1 = N/10

V_2 = Concurrent reading let X

N_2 = To be calculated

We know,

$N_1V_1 = N_2V_2$

$N2 = N_1V_1/V_2$

Result:

Strength of NaOH =_______g/mol

Precaution:

1. Always rinse burettes and pipettes with distilled water or the same solution that will be used in the experiment.
2. Use precisely calibrated glassware to ensure accurate volume measurements.
3. Do not use any glassware that is cracked or damaged.
4. Stir the solution gently and uniformly throughout the process.
5. Make sure to take burette or pipette readings at eye level for accuracy.
6. Regulate the flow of titrant carefully while adding it.
7. Ensure the titration flask is clean and completely dry before use.
8. Compare the solution's color change against a white background for better visibility.
9. Prevent the titrant level from dropping to 0 mL during the experiment.
10. If any chemical spills onto your skin, immediately wash the area thoroughly with water.

Experiment-3

Determination of chloride content of water sample by argentometric method

Theory of experiment: This method determines the chloride ion concentration of a solution by titration with silver nitrate. As the silver nitrate solution is slowly added, a precipitate of silver chloride forms.

$Ag^{+}_{(aq)} + Cl^{-}_{(aq)} \rightarrow AgCl(s) \downarrow$(White)

The end point of the titration occurs when all the chloride ions are precipitated. Then additional silver ions react with the chromate ions of the indicator, potassium chromate, to form a red-brown precipitate of silver chromate.

$2\ Ag^{+}_{(aq)} + CrO_4{}^{2-}{}_{(aq)} \rightarrow Ag_2CrO_4(s) \downarrow$(Brick red)

This method can be used to determine the chloride ion concentration of water samples from many sources such as seawater, stream water, river water and estuary water. Tap water is used as the example here. The pH of the sample solutions should be between 6.5 and 10.

Apparatus required:

Beakers, graduated cylinder, conical flask, burette, filter paper, pipette, pipette filler, volumetric flask, digital balance, Titration setup (stand, clamp, and funnel) and Stirring Rod.

Solutions and reagents:

Silver nitrate solution (0.05 M): Dissolve 8.4935 g of AR grade silver nitrate (Equivalent weight = 169.87 g/mol) in 1000 mL conical flask with distilled water and homogenize.

Potassium chromate solution (5% solution): Dissolve 5 g of AR grade potassium chromate in 100 mL of distilled water in a conical flask.

Conc. Sulphuric acid

Procedure:

- Wash the burette with distilled water and rinse with standardized solution of silver nitrate and then fill the burette with the same.

- Carefully pipette out 10 cm3 of given solution of chloride ions and transfer into a 100 cm3 conical flask. Add 1 cm3 of the potassium chromate indicator solution (it is advisable to use a 1 cm3 pipette for the purpose).

- Titrate the solution with silver nitrate solution and ensure that the flask is constantly swirled.

- With the progress of the titration, you would observe that the red colour formed by the addition of each drop of Silver nitrate begins to disappear more slowly; slow down the rate of addition of silver nitrate. The end point is indicated by sudden development of a faint but distinct change in colour to reddish-brown. This does not disappear on swirling the titration flask.

- Repeat the procedure for at least three times and record your observation in Observation Table. Determination of indicator blank

- In a clean and dry conical flask take distilled water equal to the volume of titrant + volume of the titrant and add 1 cm3 of the potassium chromate indicator solution with the help of a 1 cm3 pipette,

- Titrate the solution with silver nitrate solution while constantly stirring the flask and determine the end point as above. (As the volume of silver nitrate used for the indicator blank is going to be 70 very small you are advised to add silver nitrate drop wise right from the beginning of the titration).

- Note the volume of silver nitrate used for indicator blank and record it after the Observation Table

Observation Table:

Determination of the amount of chloride ions in the given water sample by Mohr's method:

For sample

S.No	Volume of sample solution taken(ml)	Burette reading(ml)		Vol. of $AgNO_3$ Used(ml)
		Initial	Final	
1				
2				
3				
4				

The volume of silver nitrate used for complete precipitation of chloride ions in the given solution = A cm3 =....cm3

For Blank Correction:

S.No	Volume of sample solution taken(ml)	Burette reading(ml)		Vol. of $AgNO_3$ Used(ml)
		Initial	Final	
1				
2				
3				
4				

The volume of silver nitrate used in the indicator blank titration = B cm3 =....cm3

Calculation:

The net volume of silver nitrate used for complete precipitation of chloride ions

in the given solution = (A−B) cm3 = C cm3 = ...cm3

The molarity of the chloride ions in the given solution can be determined as follows.

The reaction involved: $AgNO3 + NaCl \rightarrow AgCl(s) \downarrow + NaNO3$

Molarity equation: $M_{AgNO3} V_{AgNO3} = M_{NaCl} V_{NaCl}$

$M_{NaCl} = M_{AgNO3} . V_{AgNO3} / V_{NaCl}$

Substituting the values,

The molarity of chloride ions (as NaCl) =

The molarity of given chloride ions is = ...M

Substituting the values, of the molarity and the volume of silver nitrate used, the molarity of chloride ions is found to be: = ...M

Precautions:

1. Always rinse burettes and pipettes with distilled water or the same solution that will be used in the experiment.

2. Use precisely calibrated glassware to ensure accurate volume measurements.
3. Do not use any glassware that is cracked or damaged.
4. Stir the solution gently and uniformly throughout the process.
5. Make sure to take burette or pipette readings at eye level for accuracy.
6. Regulate the flow of titrant carefully while adding it.
7. Ensure the titration flask is clean and completely dry before use.
8. Compare the solution's color change against a white background for better visibility.
9. Prevent the titrant level from dropping to 0 mL during the experiment.
10. If any chemical spills onto your skin, immediately wash the area thoroughly with water.

Experiment-4

DETERMINATION OF DISSOLVED OXYGEN CONTENT TO WATER SAMPLE BY WINKLER'S METHOD

Theory of experiment- Oxygen dissolves in water at concentrations ranging from 7 to 9 mg/L within a temperature range of 25°C to 35°C. Measuring the dissolved oxygen content is important for assessing both the corrosive impact on boiler feed water and the extent of water pollution . The Winkler method, which uses a reagent composed of potassium bromide and potassium bromate, is commonly employed for this estimation. The water sample must be collected with care, ensuring no aeration or deaeration occurs, and stored in a ground-glass stoppered flask. To begin the test, manganous sulfate and an alkaline iodide solution are added and the reactions occur as follows

$$Mn^{2+} + 2OH^{-} \rightarrow Mn(OH)_2 \text{(white) ppt}$$

$$Mn(OH)_2 + \frac{1}{2} O_2 \rightarrow MnO(OH)_2 \text{ (Yellow brown)ppt}$$

The precipitate dissolves in concentrated sulphuric acid liberating iodine and the liberated iodine is titrated against $Na_2S_2O_3$.

$MnO(OH)_2 + 2H_2SO_4 \rightarrow Mn(SO_4)_2 + 3H_2O$
$Mn(SO_4)_2 + 2KI \rightarrow MnSO_4 + K_2SO_4 + I_2$
$Na_2S_2O_3 + I_2 \rightarrow Na_2S_4O_6 + 2NaI$

Chemical required:

1. Sodium thiosulphate solution 2. Std.Potassium dichromate solution 3. Dil H_2SO_4. 4. 5% KI 6. Starch indicator 7.Manganese sulphate 8.Alkali iodide mixture 9.Con. H_2SO_4

Apparatus Required:

1. Burette 2.pipette 3.iodine flask. 4. Iron stand

Procedure:

Titration – I

Standardization of Sodium Thiosulphate

The burette is first cleaned and rinsed with sodium thiosulphate solution, then filled with the same solution up to the zero mark. A 20 ml portion of potassium dichromate solution is transferred into a clean conical flask using a pipette. To this, 5 ml of sulphuric acid and 15 ml of 5% potassium iodide solution are added. The mixture is then titrated with the sodium thiosulphate solution. Once the solution turns a straw yellow colour, starch indicator is introduced, and titration continues. The endpoint is indicated by the disappearance of the blue colour and the development of a pale green shade. The titration is repeated until concordant readings are obtained.

Titration – II

Determination of Dissolved Oxygen

Approximately 100–150 ml of the water sample is taken in an iodine flask. To this, 2 ml of manganese sulfate and 2 ml of an alkaline iodide solution are added. The flask is stoppered, inverted, and shaken thoroughly to mix the contents. It is then allowed to stand undisturbed. Once about half of the precipitate settles, the stopper is removed, and 2 ml of concentrated sulfuric acid is added. The stopper is replaced, and the flask is inverted multiple times until the precipitate completely dissolves, forming a clear yellow solution.

Next, 20 ml of this solution is transferred to a clean conical flask and titrated with a standardized sodium thiosulfate solution. When the solution turns pale yellow, starch indicator is added. The titration continues until the blue color fades. Using the volume of sodium thiosulfate used, the concentration of dissolved oxygen is determined, and thus, the amount of dissolved oxygen in the water sample is calculated.

Observation and Calculation:

Titration – I

Std. Potassium dichromate Vs Sodium thiosulphate

S.No	**Volume of Potassium dichromate (mL)**	**Burette reading (mL)**		**Concordant volume of Sodium thiosulphate (mL)**	**Indicator**
		Initial	**Final**		
1	20				STARCH
2	20				
3	20				

Calculation:

Volume of Potassium dichromate V_1= 20mL

Strength of Potassium dichromate N_1=.............. N

Volume of Sodium thiosulphate V_2= .... mL

Strength of Sodium thiosulphate N_2= …………? ... N

According to the law of volumetric analysis

$V_1 N_1 = V_2 N_2$

$N_2 = V_1 \times N_1 / V_2$

= ……20……….. X …………….. / ……………

Strength of sodium thiosulphate N_2 =.................... N

Determination of dissolved oxygen

Titration – II

Water sample Vs Sodium thiosulphate

S.N	**Volume of water sample (mL)**	**Burette reading (mL)**		**Concordant volume of Sodium thiosulphate (mL)**	**Indicator**
		Initial	**Final**		
1	20				Starch
2	20				
3	20				

CALCULATION:

Volume of Sodium thiosulphate V_1 =.................... mL

Strength of Sodium thiosulphate N_1 =………............ N

Volume of water sample V_2 = 20 mL Strength of water sample (or)
Strength of dissolved oxygen in water N_2 = …………? .... N

According to the law of volumetric analysis

$$V_1 N_1 = V_2 N_2$$

$$N_2 = V_1 \times N_1 / V_2$$

= …………….. x …………. ... / 20

Strength of sodium thiosulphate N_2 =………............ N

Amount of dissolved oxygen in one liter of tap water = Normality x Eq.weight of oxygen x 1000 mgs

= .... N x 8 x 1000

Amount of dissolved oxygen in one liter of tap water = Normality x Eq.weight of oxygen x 1000 mgs

= .... N x 8 x 1000

Amount of dissolved oxygen in one liter of tap water =..........mgs/lit.

Result
Amount of dissolved oxygen in sample water = ……mgs/lit.

Precautions:

1. Always rinse burettes and pipettes with distilled water or the same solution that will be used in the experiment.
2. Use precisely calibrated glassware to ensure accurate volume measurements.
3. Do not use any glassware that is cracked or damaged.
4. Stir the solution gently and uniformly throughout the process.
5. Make sure to take burette or pipette readings at eye level for accuracy.
6. Regulate the flow of titrant carefully while adding it.
7. Ensure the titration flask is clean and completely dry before use.
8. Compare the solution's color change against a white background for better visibility.
9. Prevent the titrant level from dropping to 0 mL during the experiment.
10. If any chemical spills onto your skin, immediately wash the area thoroughly with water.

Experiment-5

Aim: To determine the acidity of sample water

Theory of the Experiment: Hydrogen ions that originate from the dissociation or hydrolysis of dissolved substances in a sample react with a standard sodium hydroxide (NaOH) solution. The acidity of the sample is determined based on the endpoint of the indicator used during titration.

Mineral Acidity: This is quantified by titrating the sample until it reaches a pH of approximately 3.5, which corresponds to the color change observed with methyl orange (commonly called methyl orange acidity).

Total Acidity: Determined using phenolphthalein as an indicator. The indicator changes color around pH 8.3 at 25°C, signaling the complete neutralization of carbonic acid to bicarbonate.

Apparatus Required:

1. Beaker
2. Conical flask
3. Burette
4. Pipette
5. Measuring cylinder
6. Dropper
7. Iron stand
8. Funnel

Chemicals Required:

1. Sodium hydroxide (NaOH)
2. Phenolphthalein indicator
3. Methyl orange indicator
4. Ethyl alcohol
5. Distilled water

Procedure:

1. Measure 50 ml of the sample into a conical flask and add 2–3 drops of methyl orange indicator.

2. Fill a burette with 0.02 N NaOH solution and titrate the sample until a faint orange hue appears, indicating the endpoint. Note the volume of NaOH used as V_1 (in mL).

3. To the same sample, add 2–3 drops of phenolphthalein indicator and continue the titration. When a light pink color appears, this marks the endpoint for total acidity. Record this volume as V_2 (in mL).

4. Repeat steps 1 through 3 a total of three times for consistency.

Observation and calculation:

Table -1 Mineral Acidity:

S No.	Volume of Sample (mL)	Burette Reading (mL)		Volume of NaOH (mL)	Concordant Reading
		Initial	Final		
1					
2					
3					

Burette Solution: Sodium Hydroxide

Pipette Solution: Sample

Indicator: Methyl Orange

End Point: Faint of Orange Color

Table -2

Total Acidity:

S No.	Volume of Sample (mL)	Burette Reading (mL)		Volume of NaOH (mL)	Concordant Reading
		Initial	Final		
1					
2					
3					

Burette Solution: Sodium Hydroxide

Pipette Solution: sample solution

Indicator: Phenolphthalein

End Point: Faint Pink

Calculation:

Volume of NaOH for Mineral Acidity (V_1) = V_1 mL
Volume of NaOH for Total Acidity (V_2) = V_2 mL
Normality of Sulphuric Acid= 0.02 N (let)
Volume of Sample= 100.0 mL
Equivalent weight of $CaCO_3$= 50

$$\text{Mineral Acidity} = \frac{\text{Volume of NaOH } (V_1) * N * 50 * 1000}{\text{Volume of sample taken}}$$

To convert the sample size from mL to L, multiply the result by 1,000 mL/L

Mineral Acidity as $CaCO_3$ equivalent (mg/L) =.. mg/L

$$\text{Total Acidity} = \frac{\text{Volume of NaOH } (V2) * N * 50 * 1000}{\text{Volume of sample taken}}$$

To convert the sample size from mL to L, multiply the result by 1,000 mL/L

Result:

Mineral Acidity as $CaCO_3$ equivalent (mg/L) =... mg/L
Total Acidity as $CaCO_3$ equivalent (mg/L) = … mg/L

Precaution:

1. Always rinse burettes and pipettes with distilled water or the same solution that will be used in the experiment.
2. Use precisely calibrated glassware to ensure accurate volume measurements.
3. Do not use any glassware that is cracked or damaged.
4. Stir the solution gently and uniformly throughout the process.
5. Make sure to take burette or pipette readings at eye level for accuracy.
6. Regulate the flow of titrant carefully while adding it.
7. Ensure the titration flask is clean and completely dry before use.

8. Compare the solution's color change against a white background for better visibility.
9. Prevent the titrant level from dropping to 0 mL during the experiment.
10. If any chemical spills onto your skin, immediately wash the area thoroughly with water.

Experiment no – 6

To draw pH-titration curve of strong acid vs strong base

Theory of experiment: A titration curve illustrates how the pH of a solution changes throughout a titration process. As a base is gradually added to an acidic solution, the pH rises slowly at first. However, near the equivalence point, there is a sudden and steep increase in pH. This sharp change on the curve helps identify the end point, which can then be used to determine the concentration of hydrochloric acid (HCl).

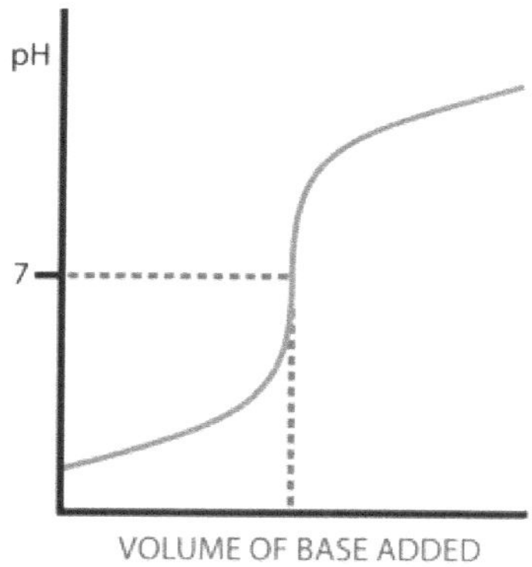

Titration curve of a strong acid (HCl) with a strong base (NaOH)

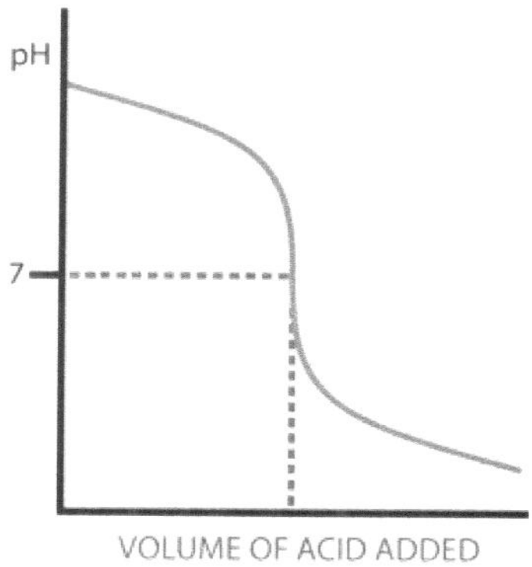

Titration curve of a strong base (NaOH) with a strong acid (HCl)

Volume of NaOH (ml)

Procedure:

1. Prepare a standard sodium hydroxide (NaOH) solution by titrating it against a 0.1 N oxalic acid solution, using phenolphthalein as the indicator.
Note: The equivalent weight of oxalic acid is 63.

2. Rinse the glass electrode thoroughly with distilled water to ensure cleanliness.

3. Measure 20 mL of hydrochloric acid (HCl) and transfer it into a 250 mL beaker. Add approximately 100 mL of distilled water so that the glass electrode can be fully submerged in the solution.

4. Record the pH of the diluted acid solution before adding any base.

5. Begin the titration by adding 1 mL of 0.1 N NaOH from a burette into the acid solution. Mix the solution well and note the pH. Continue adding NaOH in similar increments, stirring after

each addition, and record the pH after each step until about 9 to 10 mL of NaOH has been added.

6. As you approach the equivalence point, reduce the amount of NaOH added to very small volumes. Near neutralization, even an addition as small as 0.01 mL can cause a sharp rise in pH, often jumping from 9 to 10.

7. Create a titration curve by plotting pH against the volume of NaOH added (V). Also, plot a differential curve showing ΔpH/ΔV versus the average volume ($\bar{V}$), where:

$\Delta pH = pH_2 - pH_1$
$\Delta V = V_2 - V_1$
$\bar{V} = (V_1 + V_2) / 2$

Use the point of maximum slope on the curve to identify the equivalence point, and determine the volume of NaOH needed to neutralize the unknown concentration of HCl.

Observations:
Plot a graph between pH and Volume of NaOH added and a differential titration curve **ΔpH/ΔV** vs Average volume. From these two graphs, determine the volume of NaOH required for the complete neutralization of HCl.

Vol. of NaOH added (V in ml)	**pH**	**ΔV**	**ΔpH**	**ΔpH/ΔV**	**Average Vol. of NaOH added (V/ in ml)**
0		V_1-V_0	pH_1-pH_0		$(V_0 + V_1) / 2$
1		V_2-V_1	pH_2-pH_1		$(V_1 + V2) / 2$
2 contd…		contd…	contd…		contd…
3 contd…		contd…	contd…		contd…

Calculation:
For standardization of NaOH solution:
Volume of oxalic acid taken (V_1) = … ml
Strength of oxalic acid (N_1) = …. N
Volume of NaOH required (V_2) = … ml
Strength of NaOH (N_2) = ? (N)

$V_1N_1 = V_2N_2$ or $N_2 = V_1N_1 / V_2$

For calculation of the strength HCl solution:

Volume of NaOH required for complete neutralization of HCl (V_1) = -------- (ml) from graph

Strength of NaOH (N_1) = ------------ N

Volume of HCl (V_2) = ------------- (ml)

Strength of HCl (N_2) = ? (N)

Therefore Strength of HCl (N_2) = V_1N_1 / V_2

Amount = Normality x Equivalent Weight (HCl)

Amount of HCl present in the whole of the given solution = [N_2 x (Eq.wt) x 20] /1000 in gm

(Equivalent Weight of HCl = 36.5)

Result:

1. Strength of the given HCl solution = ---------- N
2. The amount of HCl present in the whole of the given solution = --------- gm

Precautions:

1. Always rinse burettes and pipettes with distilled water or the same solution that will be used in the experiment.
2. Use precisely calibrated glassware to ensure accurate volume measurements.
3. Do not use any glassware that is cracked or damaged.
4. Stir the solution gently and uniformly throughout the process.
5. Make sure to take burette or pipette readings at eye level for accuracy.
6. Regulate the flow of titrant carefully while adding it.
7. Ensure the titration flask is clean and completely dry before use.
8. Compare the solution's color change against a white background for better visibility.
9. Prevent the titrant level from dropping to 0 mL during the experiment.
10. If any chemical spills onto your skin, immediately wash the area thoroughly with water.

Experiment no-7

Determination of pH of a given sample using pH meter

Theory of experiment: The pH electrode used in the pH measurement is a combined glass electrode. It consists of sensing half-cell and reference half-cell, together form an electrode system. The sensing half-cell is a thin pH sensitive semi permeable membrane, separating two solutions, viz., the outer solution, the sample to be analyzed and the internal solution, enclosed inside the glass membrane and has a known pH value. An electrical potential is developed inside and another electrical potential is developed outside, the difference in the potential is measured and is given as the pH of the sample.

Apparatus required:

1. pH meter
2. Standard flasks
3. Magnetic Stirrer
4. Funnel
5. Beaker
6. Wash Bottle
7. Tissue Paper
8. Forceps

Chemicals required

1. Buffers Solutions of pH 4.01, 7.0 and 9.2
2. Potassium Chloride
3. Distilled Water

Procedure:

Three major steps are involved in the experiment. They are

1. Preparation of reagents
2. Calibrating the Instrument
3. Testing of Sample

Preparation of reagents

Buffer Solution of pH 4.0

2. Take 100 mL standard measuring flask and place a funnel over it.
3. Using the forceps carefully transfer one buffer tablet of pH 4.0 to the funnel.
4. Add little amount of distilled water, crush the tablet and dissolved it.
5. Make up the volume to 100 mL using distilled water.

Buffer Solution of pH 7.0

1. Take 100 mL standard measuring flask and place a funnel over it.
2. Using the forceps carefully transfer one buffer tablet of pH 7.0 to the funnel.
3. Add little amount of distilled water, crush the tablet and dissolved it.
4. Make up the volume to 100 mL using distilled water.

Buffer Solution of pH 9.2

1• Take 100 mL standard measuring flask and place a funnel over it.

2• Using the forceps carefully transfer one Buffer tablet of pH 9.2 to the funnel.

3• Add little amount of distilled water, crush the tablet and dissolved it.

4• Make up the volume to 100 mL using distilled water.

Calibrating the instrument:

Using the buffer solutions calibrate the instrument.

In a 100 mL beaker take pH 9.2 buffer solution and place it in a magnetic stirrer, insert the Teflon coated stirring bar and stir well.

Now place the electrode in the beaker containing the stirred buffer and check for the reading in the pH meter.

If the instrument is not showing pH value of 9.2, using the calibration knob adjust the reading to 9.2.

Take the electrode from the buffer, wash it with distilled water and then wipe gently with soft tissue.

If the instrument is not showing pH value of 7.0, using the calibration knob adjust the reading to 7.0.

In a 100 mL beaker take pH 7.0 buffer solution and place it in a magnetic stirrer, insert the Teflon coated stirring bar and stir well.

Now place the electrode in the beaker containing the stirred buffer and check for the reading in the pH meter.

Testing of sample:

In a 100 mL beaker take pH 4.0 buffer solution and place it in a magnetic stirrer, insert the teflon coated stirring bar and stir well.

Now place the electrode in the beaker containing the stirred buffer and check for the reading in the pH meter.

If the instrument is not showing pH value of 4.0, using the calibration knob adjust the reading to 4.0.

Take the electrode from the buffer, wash it with distilled water and then wipe gently with soft tissue. Now the instrument is calibrated.

In a clean dry 100 mL beaker take the water sample and place it in a magnetic stirrer, insert the teflon coated stirring bar and stir well.

Now place the electrode in the beaker containing the water sample and check for the reading in the pH meter. Wait until you get a stable reading.

The pH of the given water sample is 8.84

Take the electrode from the water sample, wash it with distilled water and then wipe gently with soft tissue.

Calculation:

To determine the value of pH of the given water sample the readings obtained are required to be tabulated.

Table

Sample No	Temperature of Sample (°C)	pH

Result:

For sample 1 the temperature of the measurement is ...° C and as obtained the value of the pH is....

For sample 2 the temperature of the measurement is ...° C and as obtained the value of the pH is .....

For sample 3 the temperature of the measurement is ...° C and as obtained the value of the pH is ...

Precaution:

The following precautions should be observed while performing the experiment

1. Temperature affects the measurement of pH at two points. The first is caused by the change in electrode output at different temperatures. This interference can be controlled by the instruments having temperature compensation or by calibrating the electrode-instrument system at the temperature of the samples. The second is the change of pH inherent in the sample at different temperatures. This type of error is sample dependent and cannot be controlled; hence both the pH and temperature at the time of analysis should be noted.

2. In general, the glass electrode, is not subject to solution interferences like color, high salinity, colloidal matter, oxidants, and turbidity or reluctant.

3. Oil and grease, if present in the electrode layer, should be removed by gentle wiping or detergent washing, followed by rinsing with distilled water, because it could impair the electrode response.

4. Before using, allow the electrode to stand in dilute hydrochloric acid solution for at least 2 hours.

5. Electrodes used in the pH meter are highly fragile, hence handle it carefully.

Experiment-8

Aim: Preparation of Buffer Solution and Standardization of pH Meter

Theory of experiment: A buffer solution resists changes in pH when small amounts of acid or base are added. It usually consists of:

Type of Buffer solution:

A weak acid and its salt (acidic buffer)

A weak base and its salt (basic buffer)

Examples:

Acidic buffer: Acetic acid + Sodium acetate

Basic buffer: Ammonium hydroxide + Ammonium chlorid

pH Meter Standardization:

A pH meter must be standardized before use to ensure accurate pH measurements. It is calibrated using standard buffer solutions of known pH (commonly pH 4.00, 7.00, and 9.20 or 10.00).

Apparatus required:

Beakers (100 mL, 250 mL)

Volumetric flasks

Measuring cylinder

Pipettes

Glass rod

pH meter with electrode

Distilled water

Chemicals required:

Glacial acetic acid

Sodium acetate

Ammonium hydroxide

Ammonium chloride

Standard buffer tablets/solutions (pH 4.00, 7.00, 10.00)

Distilled water

Procedure:

A.Preparation of Buffer Solutions

Acidic Buffer (pH ~4.5)

1. Take 25 mL of 0.2 M acetic acid in a beaker.
2. Add 25 mL of 0.2 M sodium acetate.
3. Mix thoroughly and transfer to a 100 mL volumetric flask.
4. Make up the volume to 100 mL with distilled water.

Basic Buffer (pH ~9.2):

1. Take 25 mL of 0.2 M ammonium hydroxide.
2. Add 25 mL of 0.2 M ammonium chloride.

Mix and make up to 100 mL in a volumetric flask with distilled water.

B.Standardization of pH Meter

Procedure:

1. Switch ON the pH meter and allow it to warm up (if necessary).
2. Rinse the electrode with distilled water and blot dry with tissue (don't rub).
3. Immerse the electrode in pH 7.00 buffer solution.
4. Adjust the meter reading to 7.00 using the calibration knob (or auto-calibrate, if digital).
5. Rinse the electrode again and immerse it in pH 4.00 or pH 10.00 buffer.
6. Adjust the second calibration knob if available (slope).
7. Rinse and store electrode in electrode storage solution or distilled water after use.

Observations Table:

A.Buffer Preparation Table:

Type of Buffer	Chemicals Used	Volume Taken	Final Volume
Acidic Buffer	0.2 M Acetic Acid + Sodium Acetate	25 mL + 25 mL	100 mL
Basic Buffer	0.2 M NH_4OH + NH_4Cl	25 mL + 25 mL	100 mL

B. pH Meter Calibration Table:

Standard Buffer Used	Actual pH	pH Meter Reading	Adjustment Done
pH 7.00	7.00		Yes/No
pH 4.00 or 10.00	4.00/10.00		Yes/No

Result:

Buffer solutions were prepared successfully.

The pH meter was standardized using pH 7.00 and pH 4.00/10.00 buffer solutions.

The meter is now ready for accurate pH measurements.

Precautions:

Use freshly prepared standard buffer solutions or certified buffer tablets.

Always rinse the electrode with distilled water before and after immersion.

Do not touch the glass bulb of the pH electrode.

Buffers and solutions should be at room temperature for accurate calibration.

Calibrate the meter at least twice with pH 7 and either 4 or 10.

Experiment no -9

Aim: Preparation of N/10 solution

Theory of experiment: Solutions of accurately known strength are called standard solutions. A standard solution contains a known weight of reagent in a definite volume of solution.

Normal solution: Normal solution is one, which contains one equivalent weight of the reagent in one liter of the solution. Normality is expressed as N.
Equivalent weight of acid= Molecular weight/ Molecular weight

Apparatus required:
Measuring Jar, Conical Flask, Weighing Bottle, Std. Flask, Pipette, Burette, and Electronic Balance.

Preparation of N/10 H_2SO_4
Equivalent weight of H_2SO_4 = 49 g
Specific gravity = 1.84 g/ml
So, volume of 49 g H_2SO_4= 26.6 ml
Concentrated H_2SO_4 (reagent grade) is about 97 per cent pure. Therefore, actual amount of concentrated H_2SO_4 required for 1.0 liter of N/10 H_2SO_4 solution = 100/97 x 26.6 = 27.42 ml
Thus, for 1.0 liter of N/10 H_2SO_4solution, 2.74 ml of concentrated H_2SO_4 is required.

Procedure:
Take 2.74 ml sulphuric acid in a beaker half-filled with distilled water.
Transfer the contents and washings to a volumetric flask (1 liter) and make volume up to the mark.
Shake well and titrate this solution with 10 ml of 0.1 N Na_2CO_3 using mixed / methyl orange as an indicator.
Repeat the titration to get at least three concordant readings. **Standardization**
Suppose 10 ml of 0.1 N Na2CO3 = 9.5 ml of H2SO4
$V_1N_1 = V_2N_2$
10 x 0.1 N = 9.5 x N = 0.10526
To prepare 1 liter N/10 H_2SO_4, the volume of 0.10526 N acid required is 1000 x 0.1/0.10526 = 950 ml.
Take 950 ml of 0.10526 N acid and dilute it to one liter. Check it again with N/10 Na_2CO_3 for three times.
It must neutralize equal volume of N/10 Na_2CO_3 solution. Label it as 0.1 N H_2SO_4.

Precautions:
Add $H_2SO_4$with the help of a burette.
Never add water to an acid.

Preparation of N/10 NaOH solution

Molecular weight of NaOH = 40 Acidity (number of replaceable OH group) = 1 Equivalent weight of NaOH = 40

Therefore, 4 g of NaOH dissolved in one liter of solution will give N/10 NaOH solution.

Procedure:

Weigh quickly 4 g NaOH in a beaker (as it is hygroscopic) and dissolve it in distilled water (preferably CO -free). Transfer the contents and the washings to a volumetric flask (1 liter). Cool and then make volume up to the mark. Shake well and standardize this solution against N/10 oxalic acid using phenolphthalein as an indicator.

Label it as 0.1 N NaOH solution.

Preparation of N/10 $KMnO_4$ solution:

Dissolve 3.2 g $KMnO_4$ in one liter of distilled water. Boil it for 10-15 minutes and then allow to stand for few days and then filter it through glass wool.

Take 10 ml of N/10 oxalic acid in a beaker. Add 5 ml dilute sulphuric acid, warm it to 60- 70°C and titrate against $KMnO_4$ from the burette till a light pinkish colour appears.

Take three concordant readings.

Suppose 10 ml 0.1 N oxalic acid = 9.75 ml of $KMnO_4$

$V_1N_1 = V_2N_2$

$10 \times 0.1\ N = 9.75 \times N_2$

Take 10 ml of N/10 oxalic acid in a beaker. Add 5 ml dilute sulphuric acid, warm it to 60- 70°C & titrate against $KMnO_4$ from the burette till a light pinkish colour appears. Take three concordant readings.

Suppose 10 ml 0.1 N oxalic acid = 9.75 ml of $KMnO_4$

$V_1N_1 = V_2N_2$

$10 \times 0.1\ N = 9.75 \times N_2$

10 x 0.1 N = ------------- = 0.10256 9.75

To prepare 1000 ml 0.1 N $KMnO_4$

100 x 9.75 x 0.1 -------------------- 10 x 0.1 solution the volume of $KMnO_4$ will be taken. Now take 975 ml of prepared $KMnO_4$ solution and make it 1000 ml by adding distilled water.

Note: Ordinary or even pure distilled water contains traces of organic matter which reduces the $KMnO_4$ solutions. That is why the solution is boiled and kept for some time before standardization. In the absence of sufficient amount of dilute H2SO4 or due to the rapid addition of $KMnO_4$ in titration flask, brown turbidity (manganous oxide) may appear.

Preparation of N/10 Na_2CO_3 solution:

Molecular weight of Na_2CO_3=106

Na_2CO_3 = 2HCl= 2NaCl+H_2O+CO_2

So, acidity of Na_2CO_3 = Equivalent weight of Na_2CO_3 = 53 Therefore, 5.3 g $Na_2CO_3$is required for each liter of solution to make N/10 Na_2CO_3.

Na2CO3 is hygroscopic, therefore, it must be made perfectly anhydrous before it is weighed out.

Procedure :

Take 6-7 g of Na_2CO_3 (A.R.) in a nickel crucible and heat it in a hot air oven at about 100°C for few hours so as to drive out any moisture and to convert any moisture and to convert any preformed $NaHCO_3$ to Na_2CO_3. Cool in a desiccator and weigh exactly 5.3 g dried salt and dissolve it in a little quantity of freshly boiled distilled water. Transfer it to one liter measuring flask and make volume up to the mark. Shake well and label it as 0.1 N

Na_2CO_3solution.

Experiment-10

Aim: Synthesis of Aspirin

Theory of experiment: Aspirin (acetylsalicylic acid) is synthesized from salicylic acid and acetic anhydride in an esterification reaction catalyzed by sulfuric acid or phosphoric acid producing Aspirin and acetic acid.

The Reaction:

Salicylic acid (C7H6O3) reacts with acetic anhydride (C4H6O3) in the presence of a catalyst (e.g., sulfuric acid, H2SO4) to form acetylsalicylic acid (aspirin, C9H8O4) and acetic acid (C2H4O2).

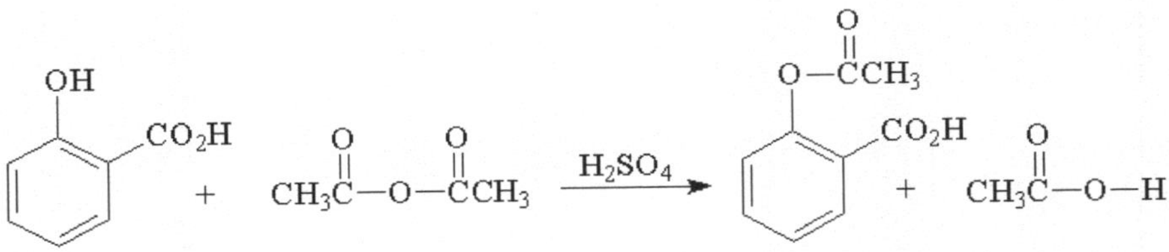

Salicylic acid   Acetic anhydride   Aspirin   Acetic acid

Apparatus required:

100 mL beaker

Filter paper

400 mL beaker

Spatula

Filter flask

Iron stand

10 mL graduated cylinder

Watch glass

Wash bottle

Buchner funnel

Stirring rod

Chemical Required:

Salicylic acid

Acetic anhydride

H_2SO_4 (concentrated) ethanol

Procedure:

1. Obtain approximately 2 g of salicylic acid and determine its mass accurately. Transfer to a 100 mL beaker.

2. Add 5 mL (0.05 mole) of acetic anhydride, followed by 5 drops of conc. H_2SO_4 (*use a dropper, H_2SO_4 is highly corrosive*) and swirl the flask gently until the salicylic acid dissolves.

3. Heat the flask gently on the steam bath (70–80°C) for at least 20-30 minutes. Use a stirring rod to get the reactants into solution. Allow the mixture to react.

4. Allow the flask to cool to room temperature. If acetylsalicylic acid does not begin to crystallize out, scratch the walls of the flask with a glass rod. Cool the mixture slightly in an ice bath until crystallization is completed. The product will appear as a solid mass when crystallization is completed.

5. Add 50 mL of water and cool the mixture in an ice bath. Do not add the water until crystal formation is complete.

6. Vacuum filter the product using a Buchner funnel. You can use some of the filtrate to rinse the Erlenmeyer flask if necessary.

7. Rinse the crystals several times with small portions (5 mL) of cold water and air dry the crystals on a Buchner funnel by suction until the crystals appear to be free of solvent. Test this crude product for the presence of unreacted salicylic acid using the ferric chloride test. Record the weight of the crude solid which probably contains water.

8. Stir the crude solid with 25 mL of a saturated aqueous sodium bicarbonate solution in a 150 mL beaker until all signs of reaction have ceased (evolution of CO_2 ceases).

9. Filter the solution through a Buchner funnel to remove any insoluble impurities or polymers that may have been formed. Wash the beaker and the funnel with 5 to 10 mL of water.

10. Carefully pour the filtrate with stirring, a small amount at a time, into an ice cold HCl solution (*ca* 3.5 mL of conc. HCl in 10 mL of water) in a 150-mL beaker and cool the mixture in an ice bath. Make sure that the resulting solution is acidic (blue litmus paper) and that the aspirin has completely precipitated out.

11. Filter the solid by suction and wash the crystals 3X with 5 mL of *cold* water each. Remove all the liquid from the crystals by pressing with a clean stopper or cork. Air dry the crystals and

transfer them to a watch glass to dry. Test a small amount of the product for the presence of unreacted salicylic acid using the ferric chloride solution.

12. When the product is completely dry, weigh the product, determine its melting point (lit mp 135-136 °C) and calculate the percentage yield.

% yield = theoretical yield/ actual yield X 100

= amount of product recovered / theoretical amount of pro

X 100

Precaution:

1. Gloves and safety goggles are mandatory when anyone is performing an experiment in the lab.
2. H_2SO_4 is corrosive in nature avoid contact with eyes, body and clothes.
3. Recording exact amounts given in manual instead of exact approximate volume/mass used.
4. Crystals have to dissolving completely during recrystallization.
5. Always wash your hands before leaving the laboratory

Experiment no-11

Aim: To prepare pure benzoic acid from toluene by oxidation using potassium permanganate.

Theory of experiment: Benzoic acid (C_6H_5COOH) is an aromatic carboxylic acid widely used in food preservation, pharmaceuticals, and dyes. It can be synthesized by the oxidation of alkyl benzene derivatives.In this experiment, toluene is oxidized by alkaline potassium permanganate to yield potassium benzoate, which upon acidification with hydrochloric acid gives benzoic acid.

Reactions :

Oxidation (in alkaline medium):

$C_6H_5CH_3 + 3[O]\ (KMnO_4, OH^-) \rightarrow C_6H_5COOK + MnO_2 + H_2O$

Acidification:

$C_6H_5COOK + HCl \rightarrow C_6H_5COOH + KCl$

The methyl group in toluene is completely oxidized to the carboxyl group, regardless of its chain length, because the benzylic carbon is highly susceptible to oxidation.

Chemicals required:

Toluene – 5 mL

Potassium permanganate ($KMnO_4$) – 8 g

Sodium hydroxide (NaOH) – 2 g

Concentrated hydrochloric acid (HCl) – \~10 mL

Distilled water – as required

Apparatus required:

250 mL round-bottom flask

Reflux condenser

Beaker (250 mL)

Funnel & filter paper

Measuring cylinder

Glass rod

Burner or heating mantle

Ice bath

Procedure:

Oxidation Step

In a round-bottom flask, add 5 mL toluene,8 g $KMnO_4$ and 2 g NaOH dissolved in 100 mL distilled water.

Fit a reflux condenser to the flask.

Heat the mixture gently under reflux for 1 hour, stirring occasionally.

Observe the gradual disappearance of purple $KMnO_4$ and formation of brown MnO_2 precipitate.

Filtration

Cool the reaction mixture slightly.

Filter the mixture to remove MnO_2 precipitate using a funnel with filter paper.

Collect the filtrate in a beaker.

Acidification:

To the filtrate, add dilute HCl dropwise with constant stirring until precipitation of benzoic acid is complete (pH $\approx$ 2).

Cool the mixture in an ice bath for 10–15 minutes to increase crystallization.

Filtration of Product

Filter the crystals of benzoic acid through a Buchner funnel or ordinary filter paper.

Wash the crystals with cold distilled water to remove any adhering acid or salts.

Drying

Transfer the crystals to a watch glass and dry them in a desiccator or at room temperature.

Observations:

Colour change: Purple $KMnO_4 \rightarrow$ brown MnO_2.

White crystalline precipitate of benzoic acid after acidification.

Crystals are needle-shaped and have a faint odour.

Result

Yield: Weigh the dried product and calculate percentage yield.

Yield = Mass of benzoic acid obtained\Theoretical mass x100

Melting point: Pure benzoic acid melts at 122 °C (check using melting point apparatus to assess purity).

Precautions:

1. Handle $KMnO_4$ carefully as it stains skin and clothes.

2. Use a fume hood when handling toluene (flammable and harmful vapour).

3. Ensure complete removal of MnO_2 before acidification.

4. Avoid overheating during reflux to prevent evaporation of toluene.

5. Cool the solution before filtration to maximize crystal formation.

Experiment no-12

Aim: To prepare nitrobenzene from benzene by nitration using a mixture of concentrated nitric acid and concentrated sulfuric acid.

Theory of experiment: Nitrobenzene ($C_6H_5NO_2$) is an aromatic nitro compound widely used in the manufacture of aniline, dyes, perfumes, and explosives. The synthesis is based on electrophilic aromatic substitution (EAS), where the nitronium ion (NO_2^+) acts as the electrophile. In the laboratory, the nitronium ion is generated in situ by the reaction of concentrated nitric acid with concentrated sulfuric acid:

Generation of nitronium ion:

$HNO_3 + 2H_2SO_4 \rightarrow NO^{2+} + H_3O^+ + 2HSO_4^-$

Overall nitration reaction:

$C_6H_6 + NO_2+ \rightarrow H_2SO_4/HNO_3 + C_6H_5NO_2 + H^+$

The reaction is highly exothermic, so temperature control (50–60 °C) is essential to avoid the formation of dinitrobenzene.

Chemicals required:

Benzene – 10 mL

Concentrated nitric acid – 10 mL

Concentrated sulfuric acid – 15 mL

Distilled water – as required

Crushed ice – for cooling

Apparatus required:

100 mL round-bottom flask

Dropping funnel

Thermometer

Water bath

Beaker (250 mL)

Glass rod

Separating funnel

Measuring cylinder

Ice bath

Reflux condenser

Procedure:

Preparation of Nitrating Mixture

1. In a beaker placed in an ice bath, take 15 mL concentrated H_2SO_4.

2. Slowly add 10 mL concentrated HNO_3 to it with constant stirring (addition of nitric acid to sulfuric acid minimizes splashing and overheating).

Nitration Reaction

3. Place 10 mL benzene in a round-bottom flask fitted with a thermometer and dropping funnel.

4. Cool the flask in an ice bath to maintain temperature below 20 °C.

5. Add the nitrating mixture drop wise to benzene while stirring, ensuring the temperature does not exceed 50–60 °C.

6. After complete addition, maintain the reaction mixture at 50–60 °C for about 30 minutes in a water bath with constant stirring.

7. Pour the reaction mixture slowly into a beaker containing crushed ice (\~100 g) to quench the reaction.

8. Transfer the mixture into a separating funnel and allow layers to separate.

9. Remove the lower aqueous acid layer and collect the upper organic layer containing crude nitrobenzene.

Purification

10. Wash the organic layer successively with:

- Cold water (to remove acids)

- Dilute sodium carbonate solution (to neutralize remaining acid)

- Again with cold water until neutral pH.

11. Dry the organic layer over anhydrous calcium chloride.

12. Distill under reduced pressure to obtain pure nitrobenzene.

Observations:

During mixing, temperature rise is noted due to the exothermic reaction.

After nitration, a pale yellow oily layer of nitrobenzene separates from the aqueous layer.

Nitrobenzene has an almond-like odour.

Result:

Appearance: Pale yellow oily liquid

Boiling point: 210–211 °C

Yield: Weigh the product and calculate the percentage yield

Yield% = Mass obtained\Theoretical mass x 100

Precautions:

1 .Handle benzene and nitrobenzene in a fume hood (both are toxic).

2. Control reaction temperature to avoid dinitration.

3. Always add acid to acid slowly when preparing nitrating mixture.

4. Wear gloves and safety goggles to avoid skin contact with corrosive acids.

5. Ensure complete washing to remove all traces of acids before distillation.

Experiment-13

Aim: To determine the Non-Carbonate Hardness of a given sample of water.

Theory of experiment: To determine permanent water hardness in a laboratory, you first need to remove temporary hardness by boiling a water sample and then titrate it with EDTA (ethylenediaminetetra acetic acid) using Eriochrome Black T as an indicator. The volume of EDTA used to reach the endpoint (wine-red to blue color change) is then used to calculate the permanent hardness.

Apparatus required:

Burette

Glass funnel

Pipette

Flask Dropper

Measuring cylinder

Conical flask

Filter paper

Chemical required:

EDTA,

Eriochrome Black-T,

NH2Cl,

Ammonia Buffer,

Magnesium Carbonate,

90% ethyl alcohol,

Distilled water.

Water sample

Procedure:

Remove Temporary Hardness:

1. Boil a known volume of the water sample (e.g., 100 ml) until approximately half the volume remains.

2. This boiling process precipitates calcium and magnesium carbonates, which cause temporary hardness.

3. Cool the solution and filter it to remove the precipitated carbonates.

4. Make up the volume of the filtrate to the original volume (100 ml) with distilled water.

Titration:

1. The burette is filled with standard EDTA solution to the zero level.
2. Take 50ml of the treated (boiled) sample water in flask. If sample having high Calcium content then take smaller volume and dilute to 50ml.
3. Add 1ml Ammonia buffer.
4. Add 5 to 6 drop of Ericrome black – T indicator. The solution turns into wine red colour.
5. Note the initial reading.
6. Titrate the content against EDTA solution. At the end point colour change from wine red to blue colour.
7. Note the final reading and record it. Repeat the process till we get concordant value. 8. Take 50ml sample in another flask and boiled it. (Add distilled water to get final volume of water.)
9. Repeat step 3-7.

Calculations:

S.No	Water sample (50ml)	Initial Value	Final Value	Ml of EDTA
1				x
2				
3				

Permanent Hardness (mg/L as CaCO3) = (Volume of EDTA used x Molarity of EDTA x 100,000) / Volume of water sample (in ml)

Result: Permanent Hardness (mg/L as CaCO3) =...........

Precaution:

1. Distilled water was used for washing and rinsing of glass apparatus.
2. Same amount of indicator was added each time.
3. pH 10 was maintained during the titration by adding buffer.
4. End point was observed carefully.

Experiment-14

Aim: To determine the Carbonate Hardness of a given sample of water.

Theory of experiment: Carbonate and bicarbonate ions in the sample can be determined by titrating it with against slandered sulphuric acid (H_2SO_4) using phenolphthalein and methyl orange as indicators. Addition of phenolphthalein gives pink red colour in presence of carbonates and titration with H_2SO_4 convert CO_3^{2-}into $HCO_3^{-}$and decolorise the red colour as shown below

$Na_2Co_3 + H2SO4 \rightarrow 2NaHCO_3 + Na_2\ SO4$

Thus the carbonate neutralization is only half way these carbonate along with already present ones are then determined by continuing the titration using methyl orange indicator which gives yellow colour in presence of bicarbonate. On complete neutralization of bicarbonate the yellow colour will change to red.

$2NaOHCO_3 + H_2SO_4 \dashrightarrow Na_2SO_4 + 2H_2O + CO_2$

The bicarbonate titre value will be less since carbonate is not present.

Apparatus required:

Burette

Glass funnel

Pipette

Flask Dropper

Measuring cylinder

Conical flask

Chemical required:

Sulphric acid (.1N)

Water sample

Phenol naphthalene

Methyl orange

Procedure:

1. Pipette out 10 ml of sample water in conical flask.
2. Add 1or 2 drop of phenol naphthalene, the solution will turn pink colour
3. Titrate the contents against the 0.1N H_2SO_4 filled in burette, the end point is indicated by change in pink colour to colourless. Record the burette reading.
4. If on addition of phenol naphthalene the sample does not change to pink, it indicates the absence of CO_3^{2-} .
5. In such case add methyl orange indicator in the same aliquot and titrate against the 0.1N H_2SO_4 till the straw yellow colour changes to rose red.
6. Note the burette reading.

Table:

S.N.	Volume of H_2SO_4 consumed for neutralization of CO_3^{2-} (ml)	Volume of H_2SO_4 consumed for neutralization of HCO_3^- (ml)	meq/l HCO_3^-	meq/l CO_3^{2-}
1				
2				
3				
4				

Calculation:

Amount of 0.1N H2SO4 consumed in 1st titration = A ml

Amount of 0.1N H2SO4 consumed in 2nd titration = B ml

Amount of carbonate ion meq/l= 20 x A

Amount of bicarbonate ion meq/l= 20x (A-B)

Result:

The carbonate and bicarbonate in given water --------- meq/l

Precautions:

1. Distilled water was used for washing and rinsing of glass apparatus.
2. Same amount of indicator was added each time.
3. pH 10 was maintained during the titration by adding buffer .
4. End point was observed carefully.

Experiment-15

Aim: To determine the total Hardness of a given sample of water by EDTA method.

Theory of experiment: Hardness in water is due to the presence of dissolved salts of calcium and magnesium. Hardness is caused by polyvalent metallic cations, though the divalent cations, such as calcium and magnesium cations are usually the predominant cause of hardness. In addition, hardness is also caused by Fe2+ and Mn2+ ions. For example, when hard water is heated, Ca2+ ions react with bicarbonate (HCO3 -) ions to form insoluble calcium carbonate (CaCO3).

$Ca^{+2}_{(aq)} + 2HCO_3^-{}_{(aq)} \rightarrow CaCO_{3(s)} + H_2O + CO_2$

$Mg^{2+}{}_{(aq)} + 2OH^{--} \rightarrow Mg(OH)_{2(s)}$

Depends on ability of ethylenediamine tetra acetic acid (C10H16O8N2) or its disodium salt to form stable complexes with calcium and magnesium ions. When the dye eriochrome black T (EBT) (C2OH13.N3O7S) is added to solution containing calcium and magnesium ions at pH 10.0, a Wine red complex is formed, this solution is titrated with standard solution of disodium salt of EDTA, which extracts calcium and magnesium from the dye complex and the dye is changed back to its original blue colour. Eriochrome black T is used to indicate the end point for the titration of calcium and magnesium together.

Apparatus required:

Burette 25-30ml

Glass funnel

Pipette 1ml

Flask Dropper

Measuring cylinder

Conical flask

Chemical required:

EDTA,

Eriochrome Black-T,

NH2CL,

Ammonia Buffer,

Magnesium Carbonate,

90% ethyl alcohol,

Distilled water,

Water sample,

Reagent preparation:

1. EDTA solution: 4gm EDTA and 0.1gm magnesium bicarbonate dissolve in 800 ml distilled water.
2. Eriochrome Black-T: 0.4gm Ericrome Black T, 4.5 gm hydroxylmine hydrochloride add in 100ml 95% ethyl alcohol.

3. Ammonia Buffer:

Stock A: 16.9gm of NH_4CL in 143ml of conc. NH_4CH,

Stock B: 1.25gm magnesium salt of EDTA dissolve in 50 ml distilled water. Mix both stock solutions and dilute to 250ml with DDW. Dilute 10ml of the solution to 100ml with DDW.

Procedure:

1. The burette is filled with standard EDTA solution to the zero level.
2. Take 50ml sample water in flask. If sample having high Calcium content then take smaller volume and dilute to 50ml.
3. Add 1ml Ammonia buffer.
4. Add 5 to 6 drop of Ericrome black – T indicator. The solution turns into wine red colour.
5. Note the initial reading.
6. Titrate the content against EDTA solution. At the end point colour change from wine red to blue colour.
7. Note the final reading and record it. Repeat the process till we get concordant value. 8. Take 50ml sample in another flask and boiled it. (Add distilled water to get final volume of water.)
9. Repeat step 3-7.

Calculations:

S.No	Water sample (50ml)	Initial Value	Final Value	Ml of EDTA
1				x
2				
3				

Total hardness of water mg/L ($CaCO_3$ Scale) = ml of EDTA used (unboiled) 1000 /ml of sample

Or,

Hardness (in mg/L as $CaCO_3$) = $(V \times N \times 50 \times 1000) / (SV)$

Where:

V = volume of titrant (mL); N = normality of EDTA; 50 = equivalent weight of $CaCO_3$; SV = sample volume (mL)

Permanent hardness of water mg/L ($CaCO_3$ Scale) = ml of EDTA used (boiled) 1000/ml of sample

Temporary hardness of water mg/L ($CaCO_3$ Scale) = Total hardness of water - Permanent hardness of water

1000 ml of 1(M) EDTA ≡ 100 gm $CaCO_3$

1 ml of 1(M) EDTA ≡ (100/1000) gm $CaCO_3$

1 ml of 1(M/50) EDTA ≡ (100/1000) × (1/50) gm

$CaCO_3$ ≡ (100/1000) × (1/50) × 1000 mg $CaCO_3$ ≡ 2 mg $CaCO_3$

x ml of EDTA required for titration So,

x ml (M/50) EDTA ≡ 2 × x = 2x mg $CaCO_3$

Now Volume of water taken = 50 ml so,

50 ml water contains = 2xmg $CaCO_3$

1000 ml water contains = [2x/50 × 1000] mg $CaCO_3$ = y ppm or mg/l

Observation:

The colour of soluble distilled water and R.O water instantly changed into blue while tap water and pond water turned wine red when Ericrome black T was added and therefore after turned blue when titrated against EDTA solution.

Precautions:

1. Distilled water was used for washing and rinsing of glass apparatus.
2. Same amount of indicator was added each time.
3. pH 10 was maintained during the titration by adding buffer .
4. End point was observed carefully.

Experiment-16

Aim: Estimation of Mohr's salt using standard KMnO4.

Theory of experiment: Potassium permanganate is a strong oxidant in the presence of sulfuric acid. Mohr salt is a double salt forming a single crystalline structure having the formula $FeSO_4.(NH_4)_2SO_4.6H_2O$. The chemical name for Mohr's salt is ferrous ammonium sulfate.

Mohr salt acts as a reducing agent and potassium permanganate acts as an oxidizing agent. Acid Base Titration with Mohr's Salt against KMnO4 is an example of redox reaction. In this redox reaction, ferrous ion from Mohr's salt gets oxidized and pink colored of manganese present in potassium permanganate, which is in the +7-oxidation state gets reduced to colorless Mn^{2+} state.

The chemical reaction and the molecular chemical equation is given below.

Reduction half reaction –

$$2KMnO_4 + 3H_2SO_4 \rightarrow K_2SO_4 + 2MnSO_4 + 3H_2O + 5[O]$$

Oxidation half reaction –

$$[2FeSO_4 (NH_4)_2SO_4.6H_2O + H_2SO_4 + [O] \rightarrow Fe_2 (SO_4)_3 + 2(NH_4)_2SO_4 + 13H_2O] \times 5$$

Overall reaction –

$$2KMnO_4 + 10FeSO_4 (NH_4)_2SO_4.6H_2O + 8H_2SO_4 \rightarrow K_2SO_4 + 2MnSO_4 + 5Fe_2 (SO_4)_3 + 10(NH_4)_2SO_4 + 68H_2O$$

Apparatus required:

Burette

Conical Flask

Beakers

Pipette

Funnel

Retort Stand with Clamp

Measuring flask

Volumetric flask

Chemical Required:

1. Mohr's salt

2. Potassium permanganate

3. Sulfuric acid

Procedure:

Preparation of 250ml of M/20 solution of Mohr's salt:

1. The molar mass of Mohr's salt is 392gmol^{-1}. It is a primary standard. Since 1000cm^3 of 1M potassium permanganate require Mohr's salt of =392g So, 250cm^3 of M/20 potassium permanganate require Mohr's salt of = $(392 / 20) / 1000 \times 250 = 4.9$g
2. Accurately weigh 4.9g of Mohr's salt using a chemical balance and watch glass.
3. Now put weighed Mohr's salt in a volumetric flask using a funnel.
4. Now add 5ml of dilute sulfuric acid and distilled water in the same flask and dissolve Mohr's salt.
5. Now fill the volumetric flask with distilled water according to the required volume.

Titration

1. Wash the pipette and the burette with distilled water and then rinse it with the corresponding solution which needs to be filled in them.
2. Rinse the burette with potassium permanganate solution and then fill the potassium permanganate solution in it.
3. Fix the burette in the burette stand and then place a white tile beneath it so that the endpoint can easily be traced.
4. Rinse the pipette as well as the conical flask with Mohr's salt.
5. Take out 10 ml of standard more mohr salt solution in the conical flask.
6. Add 1 + 2 full of sulfuric acid so as to prevent the oxidation of manganese to form manganese dioxide.
7. Take the initial reading of the burette before starting that experiment.
8. Now against the potassium permanganate solution start the titration and slowly still the flask gently.
9. Initially, the purple colour of $KMnO_4$ will be discharged with ferrous ammonium sulfate. The appearance of the permanent pink colour indicates the endpoint. Repeat the experiment unless 3 concordant value is obtained.
10. It is important to note down the upper meniscus reading of the burette

Observation Table:

S.N.	Vol. of Mohr's salt solution(ml)	Strength of KMnO4 (N)	Burette reading of KMnO4 (ml)			concordant value
			Initial (ml)	Final (ml)	Difference	
1						
2						
3						
4						

Calculation:

Strength of Fe2+ in Mohr's salt solution: Volume of KMnO4 solution required for Mohr's salt solution = a ml = ...ml.

Strength of KMnO4 solution = y (N) = ... (N).

a ml of y(N) KMnO4 solution ≡ 55.85 X a X y/1000gm of Fe2+

≡ z gm of Fe2+ = ...gm.

1000ml of Mohr's salt contain = z X 1000/5 gm of Fe2+ = ... gm. = w gm of Fe2+ Amount of Fe2+ = w gm /lit = ... gm./ lit

Conclusion:

The amount of Fe2+ estimated in the supplied Mohr's salt solution is .... gms. /lit at ....0C.

Experiment-17

Aim: To determine the strength of a given Potassium dichromate solution with N/20sodium thiosulphate (Hypo) solution

Theory of experiment: This is an iodometric titration, where liberated iodine is titrated with thiosulphate. The reaction involves potassium dichromate oxidizing iodide ions to iodine, which is then reduced by thiosulphate. Potassium dichromate is a strong oxidizing agent. In acidic medium, it liberates iodine from potassium iodide (KI). The liberated iodine is then titrated against standard sodium thiosulphate solution.

Reaction involve:

$K_2Cr_2O_7 + 7H_2SO_4 + 6KI \rightarrow 4K_2SO_4 + Cr_2(SO)_4 + 7H_2O + 3I_2$

$2Na_2S_2O_3 + I_2 \rightarrow Na_2S_4O_2 + 2NaI$

Hence

$K_2Cr_2O_7 = 3I_2 + 6\ Na_2S_2O_3$

Apparatus required:

Burette

Pipette (25 mL)

Conical flask

Measuring cylinder

Beaker

Funnel

Chemicals required:

Given potassium dichromate solution

N/20 sodium thiosulphate solution

Potassium iodide (KI)

Dilute sulphuric acid or hydrochloric acid

Freshly prepared starch solution (indicator)

Distilled water

Procedure:

1. Rinse and fill the burette with N/20 sodium thiosulphate solution.
2. Pipette out 25.0 mL of the given potassium dichromate solution into a clean conical flask.
3. Add about 10 mL of 10% KI solution and 5–10 mL of dilute $H_2SO_4$to the conical flask.
4. Allow the solution to stand for 1–2 minutes in the dark (to ensure complete liberation of iodine).
5. Titrate the liberated iodine with sodium thiosulphate solution from the burette.
6. When the solution becomes pale yellow, add 2–3 mL of starch solution (the solution turns deep blue).

7. Continue titrating until the blue color just disappears (end point).

8. Note the burette reading.

9. Repeat the experiment to obtain concordant value (i.e., at least 3 consistent readings).

Observations Table:

S.No	Volume of Dichromate (mL)	Burette Reading (ml)			Concordant reading
		Initial Reading (mL)	Final Reading (mL)	Difference	
1	25.0				
2	25.0				
3	25.0				

Calculations:

Let the average volume of sodium thiosulphate used = V mL

Normality of sodium thiosulphate (N_1) = 1/20 = 0.05 N

Volume of sodium thiosulphate = V mL

Volume of potassium dichromate = 25.0 mL

Normality of potassium dichromate = N_2

$N_1V_1 = N_2V_2 \Rightarrow 0.05 \times V = N_2 \times 25$

$\Rightarrow N_2 = 0.05 \times V/25$

Strength (g/L) = Normality × Equivalent weight of $K_2Cr_2O_7$

Equivalent weight of $K_2Cr_2O_7$ = 49.03 g/eq

So,

Strength = $N_2 \times 49.03 = 0.05 \times V/25 \times 49.03$

Result:

The strength of the given potassium dichromate solution is= .... g/L

Precautions:

Use freshly prepared starch solution.

Perform titration immediately after adding KI to prevent iodine loss.

Rinse the pipette, burette, and conical flask properly before use.

Avoid direct sunlight during titration (iodine is volatile).

Use white tile to observe the color change clearly.

Experiment-18

Aim: To Determine the Strength of Silver Ions (Ag^+) in a Given $AgNO_3$ Solution Using Chloride Ions (Mohr's Method)

Theory of experiment: This is a precipitation titration method called Mohr's method. It is based on the formation of a white precipitate of silver chloride (AgCl) when silver nitrate reacts with sodium chloride. Once all Ag^+ has reacted, the first excess of Cl^- reacts with chromate ions to form a reddish-brown precipitate of silver chromate (Ag_2CrO_4), indicating the end point.

Titration reaction

$AgNO_3 + NaCl \rightarrow AgCl + NaNO_3$

End point reaction:

$2Ag^+ + CrO_4^{2-} \rightarrow Ag_2CrO_4 \downarrow$ reddish-brown ppt

Apparatus required:

Burette

Pipette (25 mL)

Conical flask

Measuring cylinder

Beakers

Funnel

Chemicals required:

Given $AgNO_3$ solution (unknown concentration)

Standard NaCl solution (e.g., N/50 or 0.02 N)

Potassium chromate indicator (K_2CrO_4)

Distilled water

Procedure:

Rinse and fill the burette with standard NaCl solution.

Pipette out 25.0 mL of the Ag NO_3 solution into a conical flask.

Add 1–2 mL of potassium chromate solution as the indicator (solution turns yellow).

Titrate slowly with NaCl solution from the burette.

Near the endpoint, a reddish-brown precipitate of Ag_2CrO_4 appears and persists (does not disappear on shaking).

Note the burette reading.

Repeat the titration to obtain concordant readings (at least 2-3 consistent values).

Observations Table:

S.No	Volume of $AgNO_3$ (mL)	Initial Burette Reading (mL)	Final Burette Reading (mL)	Volume of NaCl used (mL)
1	25.0			
2	25.0			
3	25.0			

Calculations

Let the average volume of NaCl used = V mL

Normality of NaCl (N_1) = e.g., 0.02 N

Volume of NaCl = V mL

Volume of $AgNO_3$ = 25.0 mL

Normality of $AgNO_3$ = N_2

$N_1 \times V = N_2 \times 25 \rightarrow N_2 = N_1 \times V/25$

Strength (g/L) = Normality × Equivalent weight of $AgNO_3$

Equivalent weight of $AgNO_3$ = Molar mass = 169.87 g/mol (since it gives 1 Ag^+ ion per mole)

Strength = $N_2 \times 169.87 = N_1 \times V/25 \times 169.87$

Result:

The strength of silver ions (Ag^+) in the given $AgNO_3$ solution is = ... g/L

Precautions:

1. Perform the titration in neutral to slightly alkaline medium (Mohr's method is pH-sensitive).
2. Use freshly prepared potassium chromate indicator.
3. Rinse the pipette and burette properly before use.
4. The reddish-brown Ag_2CrO_4 precipitate should appear gradually and persist.
5. Avoid over titration; stop at first permanent pink/brown color.

Experiment no-19

Aim: Estimation of Barium as Barium Sulphate (Gravimetric Method)

Theory of experiment: This is a gravimetric analysis method. Barium ions (Ba^{2+}) are quantitatively precipitated from a barium salt solution (like $BaCl_2$) by adding excess sulphuric acid (H_2SO_4) or sulphate ions (e.g., from H_2SO_4 or Na_2SO_4) to form barium sulphate ($BaSO_4$), a white insoluble precipitate.

$Ba^{2+} + SO_4^{2-} \rightarrow BaSO_4 \downarrow$ppt

The precipitate is filtered, washed to remove impurities, dried, ignited (if necessary), and weighed. From the mass of $BaSO_4$, the amount of Ba^{2+} can be calculated using stoichiometry.

Apparatus required:

Beakers

Glass rod

Measuring cylinder

Funnel

Filter paper (Whatman No. 42 or equivalent)

Gooch crucible or sintered glass crucible (or porcelain crucible)

Balance

Oven and desiccator

Chemicals required:

Barium chloride ($BaCl_2$) solution (given sample)

Dilute sulphuric acid (H_2SO_4) or sodium sulphate (Na_2SO_4) solution

Distilled water

Procedure:

Take 50 mL of the barium chloride solution in a beaker.

Heat the solution to about 60–70°C.

Slowly add dilute sulphuric acid (or Na_2SO_4 solution) dropwise with constant stirring until precipitation is complete.

Allow the precipitate of $BaSO_4$ to settle.

Digest the precipitate for 30 minutes on a water bath or low flame to ensure complete and compact precipitation.

Filter the precipitate using pre-weighed filter paper or crucible.

Wash the precipitate several times with hot distilled water to remove chloride/sulphate ions (test the washings with $AgNO_3$ for Cl^- or $BaCl_2$ for SO_4^{2-}).

Dry the filter paper with precipitate in an oven at 110°Cuntil constant weight is obtained.

Cool in a desiccator and weigh accurately.

Record the mass of $BaSO_4$ obtained.

Observations and Calculations:

Description	Mass (g)
Weight of filter paper/crucible (W_1)	
Weight of filter paper + $BaSO_4$ (W_2)	
Mass of $BaSO_4 = W_2 - W_1$	

Molar Masses:

Molar mass of $BaSO_4$ = 233.39 g/mol

Molar mass of Ba = 137.33 g/mol

Amount of Ba = 137.33 /233.39 x times mass of $BaSO_4$

Strength of Ba^{2+} in g/L (if solution volume used = V mL):

Strength (g/L) = mass of Ba in g/ V x 1000

Result:

Mass of Barium Sulphate ($BaSO_4$) obtained = ... g

Amount of Barium (Ba^{2+}) present in the given solution = ... g

Strength of Ba^{2+} in the sample solution = ... g/L

Precautions:

1. Add sulphuric acid slowly to avoid super-saturation and colloidal precipitate.
2. Ensure complete precipitation by allowing the mixture to stand or digest.
3. Use hot water for washing to avoid dissolution of $BaSO_4$.
4. Dry the precipitate completely to obtain accurate weight.
5. Handle the filter paper carefully to avoid tearing and loss of precipitate.

Experiment no-20

Aim: Qualitative Analysis of One Cation and One Anion in a given salt

Theoryof experiment: Qualitative analysis is based on the selective precipitation and characteristic reactions of ions. The analysis involves:

Preliminary tests (physical properties, solubility, flame test, etc.)

Systematic group analysis for cations

Confirmatory tests for anions

Cations and Anions under Study

CationsPb^{2+}, Cu^{2+}, Al^{3+}, Fe^{3+}, Mn^{2+}, Ni^{2+}, Zn^{2+}, Co^{2+}, Ca^{2+}, Sr^{2+}, Ba^{2+}, Mg^{2+}, NH_4^+

AnionsCO_3^{2-}, S^{2-}, NO_2^-, SO_3^{2-}, SO_4^{2-}, NO_3^-, Cl^-, Br^-, I^-, PO_4^{3-}, $C_2O_4^{2-}$, CH_3COO^-

Apparatus required:

Test tubes, test tube holder, and dropper

Glass rod, beaker, and burner

Filter paper, watch glass

Chemicals required:

Dil. and conc. HCl, H_2SO_4, HNO_3, NaOH, NH_4OH, $BaCl_2$, $AgNO_3$, $KMnO_4$, Nessler's reagent, etc.

Group reagents: HCl, H_2S, NH_4Cl, NH_4OH, Na_2CO_3

Known reagents for confirmatory tests

Procedure:

Step A: Preliminary Examination

1. Physical appearance – Note the color, smell, and texture of the salt.

2. Flame test (for cations like Ba^{2+}, Sr^{2+}, Ca^{2+}) – Observe flame color.

3. Dry heating test – Heat a small quantity of salt in a dry test tube.

Observe evolution of gases or color change.

Step B: Detection of Anion (Acid Radicals)

1. Prepare sodium carbonate extract.

Boil 1g salt with 10 mL distilled water + sodium carbonate.

Filter and collect the filtrate for anion testing.

2. Perform group tests for anions:

Add dil. HCl: Effervescence → CO_3^{2-}

Add $BaCl_2$ solution: White ppt → SO_4^{2-} (insoluble in HCl), SO_3^{2-} (soluble in HCl)

Add $AgNO_3$: White ppt → Cl^-, Yellow ppt → I^-

Add $FeSO_4$ + conc. H_2SO: Brown ring → NO_3^-
Add $KMnO_4$: Decolorization → S^{2-}, SO_3^{2-}, NO_2^-, $C_2O_4^{2-}$
Add ammonium molybdate + HNO_3: Yellow ppt → PO_4^{3-}
Add ferric chloride: Blood red color → $C_2O_4^{2-}$ or CH_3COO^-

3. Confirmatory tests based on suspected anion.

Step C: Detection of Cation (Basic Radicals)

1. Prepare original solution:
Dissolve a pinch of salt in distilled water or dil. HCl.
2. Group-wise cation analysis:

Group	Group Reagent	Radicals Detected
I	Dil. HCl	Pb^{2+}, Ag^+
II	H_2S in acidic medium	Cu^{2+}, Pb^{2+}
III	NH_4Cl +NH_4OH + H_2S	Al^{3+}, Fe^{3+}, Mn^{2+}, Cr^{3+}
IV	NH_4OH + H_2S	Ni^{2+}, Co^{2+}, Zn^{2+}
V	$(NH_4)_2CO_3$ + NH_4OH	Ca^{2+}, Ba^{2+}, Sr^{2+}
VI	No group ppt	Mg^{2+}, NH_4^+

3. **Confirmatory tests for identified cation**:

Pb^{2+}: Yellow ppt with KI
Cu^{2+}: Blue ppt with NH_4OH
Fe^{3+}: Blood red with KSCN
Al^{3+}: White gelatinous ppt with NH_4OH
Mn^{2+}: Pink ppt with NaOH
Ni^{2+}: Red ppt with dimethylglyoxime
Zn^{2+}: White ppt with NaOH, dissolves in excess
Ca^{2+}: White ppt with $(NH_4)_2CO_3$
Ba^{2+}: White ppt with H_2SO_4 ($BaSO_4$)
Sr^{2+}: White ppt with $(NH_4)_2SO_4$
Mg^{2+}: White ppt with NaOH
NH_4^+: Ammonia gas with NaOH + heat → pungent smell

Observation Table:

Test	Observation	Inference
Physical appearance		
Dry heating test		
Flame test		
Anion group test		Suspected anion
Confirmatory test for anion		Anion confirmed
Cation group test		Suspected cation group
Confirmatory test for cation		Cation confirmed

Result:

Cation detected: ....

Anion detected: ....

Hence, the given salt is [name of salt]

Precautions:

1. Use dilute acids carefully to avoid excessive reaction.
2. Wash test tubes properly between tests to avoid contamination.
3. Handle toxic gases (like H_2S) in a fume chamber.
4. Use freshly prepared reagents for accurate results.
5. Record observations carefully and do not assume results.

Experiment-21

Determination of surface tension and Viscosity

Aim: Determine the surface tension of a given liquid at room temp using stalgmometer by drop number method

Requirements: Stalgmometer, specific gravity bottle, a small rubber tube with a screw pinch cork, distilled water, experimental liquid.

Theory of experiment: In the drop number method, the number of drops formed by equal volumes of two liquid is counted. If m1 and m2 is the mass of one drop of each of the liquid having densities d1 and d2 respectively. If n1 and n2 is the number of drops formed by volume v of the two liquids, then their surface tensions are related as

$¥_1/¥_2 = (d_1/d_2)*(n_2/n_1)$

One of the liquid is water its surface tension and density are known. Then surface tension of the given liquid can be calculated.

Procedure:

1. Clean the stalgmometer with chromic acid mix, wash with water and dry it
2. Attach a small piece of rubber tube having a screw pinch cock at the upper end of the stalgmometer. 3. Immerse the lower end of the stalgmometer in distilled water and suck the water 1-2cm above mark A. adjust the pinch cork so that 10-15 drops fall per minute
4. Clamp the stalgmometer allow the water drops to fall and start counting the number of drops when the meniscus crosses the upper mark A and stop counting when the meniscus passes mark B
5. Repeat the exercise to take three to four readings
6. Rinse the stalgmometer with alcohol and dry it
7. Suck the given liquid in the stalgmometer and count the drops as in case of water
8. Take a clean dry weighing bottle weighs it with water as well as with liquid.
9. Note the temp of water taken in a beaker.

Observations:

Room temp=t ^{0}C

Density of water=dw

Surface tension of water=¥ dynes/cm

No of drops From a Fixed Volume				Mean
Liquid	1	2	3	nl=
Water	1	2	3	nw=

Weight of empty specific gravity bottle=$w_1$gram

Weight of specific gravity bottle+water=w_2 gram

Weight of empty sp.gravity bottle+liquid=$w_3$gram

Weight of water= (w_2-w_1) gram

Weight of liquid= (w_3-w_1) gram

Calculations:

Density of the liquid

$D_l= (w_3-w_1)/(w_2-w_1)*dw$

Surface tension of liquid=

¥l/¥w = (d_l/dw)*(n_w/n_l)* ¥w

Result:

The surface tension of liquid is ....dynes/cm.

Precaution:

1. Ensure they are thoroughly cleaned with caustic soda and water to remove any contaminants that could affect surface tension measurements.
2. Clean and dry the stalagmometer before use.
3. Carefully clean the dish to avoid any dirt or residue.
4. Remove any dirt or residue from the metal ring used in some experiments.
5. Keep the capillary tube vertical while dripping in water.
6. Hold the stalagmometer in a vertical position throughout the drop counting process.
7. Maintain a constant and known temperature during the experiment.
8. Measure the height of the liquid column from the lowest point of the meniscus.
9. Observe carefully when the water and liquid are just passing the upper and lower marks of the stalagmometer.

Experiment-22

Determination of the rate constant of a reaction

Aim: To study the kinetics of acid-catalyzed hydrolysis of ethyl acetate and to evaluate the value of the rate constant.

Theory of experiment:

A first order reaction is one in which the rate depends on concentration of only one of the reactants. Methyl acetate hydrolyses, in the presence of an acid, which acts as a catalyst, to give acetic acid and methyl alcohol.

$$CH_3COOCH_3 + H_2O \xrightarrow{\text{Dil. acid}} CH_3COOH + CH_3OH$$

Methyl acetate　　　　Acetic acid　　methyl alcohol

Rate = k'$[CH_3COOCH_3]\,[H_2O]$

Where k' is the specific reaction rate constant. Since water is present in large excess, its concentration remains practically constant throughout the reaction. As a result of this assumption, the above equation reduces to

Rate= k' $[CH_3COOCH_3]$

Where k' = k $[H_2O]$ = Constant

Hence, the rate of reaction is determined by the first power of the concentration of the ester and so the reaction is of the first order. It is however, a pseudo first order reaction which is not first order but is forced to obey the first order rate expression. Such reactions involve more than one molecule in the chemical reaction. As acetic acid is produced during the hydrolysis of methyl acetate, the reaction can be followed by titrating the reaction mixture with standard solution of an alkali.

The value of k can be calculated according to the first order rate expression which is given by,

$$k = \frac{2.303}{t} \times \log \frac{a}{a - x} \quad \text{[or]}$$

$$k = \frac{2.303}{t} \times \log \frac{V_\infty - V_0}{V_\infty - V_t}$$

Where,
V_o = Volume of alkali used at t = 0 min,
V_t = Volume of alkali used at any time of reaction,
V_∞ = Volume of alkali used at the end of the reaction.

The values of rate constant can be calculated at different intervals of time t. It is independent of the initial concentration of the ester. It has the dimensions of time^{-1}. Calculate the k_t for each reading with respect to time and determine the calculated average k of the reaction. Plot a graph (straight line through origin) of log V_∞ - V_0/ V_∞ - V_t against (t) and from the slope determine the rate constant k = slope x 2.303.

Apparatus required:

1. Measuring cylinder
2. Pipette
3. Burette
4. Conical Flask
5. Stop watch

Material required:

N/10 NaOH

N/20 HCL

Phenolphthalein indicator

Procedure:

1. Take 25ml of cold water in a 250 ml conical flask. Add 4-5 drops of phenolphthalein indicator to it.
2. Take 50ml of N/20 HCL in a separate 100 ml conical flask. Add 5ml of ethyl acetate to it. Quickly shake the reaction mixture for few seconds and note the time because reaction starts. Immediately pipette out exact 5ml of reaction mixture take in the conical flask containing cold water and indicator.
3. Immediately titrate the mixture against N/10 NaOH solution in burette up to end point (pink colour) persisting for 20-30 seconds. Note down the titre value V_o.
4. Repeat the same operation and titration at every 10 minutes until 50th minute of the reaction. The titre value in such cases will be V_t.
5. Finally, heat the reaction mixture at 70^0-80^0C for 10-15 minutes to complete the reaction. And then once again take 5ml of the reaction mixture and titrate it to get V_∞.

Observations:

Sl. No.	**Time (min)**	**Burette Reading (ml)**		**Vol. of NaOH (ml)**	$\log\frac{V_\infty - V_O}{V_\infty - V_t}$	**k (min^{-1})**
		Initial	**Final**			

1	0			(value =V0)		
2	10					
3	20					
4	30					
5	40					
6	50					
7	60					
8	∞			(value =V∞)		
Calculated average rate constant (k_{av})=						

Calculation:

1. Complete the calculation as per table.
2. Draw the plot and calculate k_{plot}

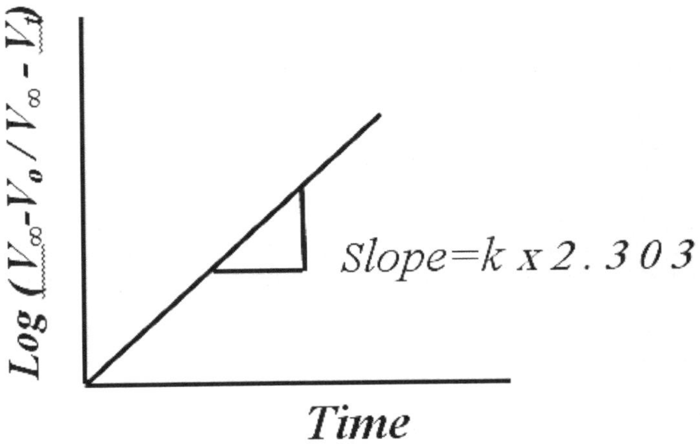

Result:

From the linear nature of the plot, the order of the reaction was confirmed as 1 (pseudo first order). For the reaction the k_{av}=......... and k_{plot}= ....

Precautions:

1. Used fresh and accurately measured reagents.
2. Standardized the reagent used.
3. Maintained constant temperature.
4. Ensure rapid cooling of samples for titration to minimize further reaction.

Experiment-23

Adsorption of acetic acid by charcoal

Aim: Determination of adsorption isotherm of acetic acid on activated charcoal

Theory of experiment: Adsorption is a process that occurs when a gas or liquid solute accumulates on the surface of a solid or a liquid (adsorbent), forming a molecular or atomic film (adsorbate). There are two type of adsorption:

Physisorption is a type of adsorption in which the adsorbate adheres to the surface only through Van der Waals (weak intermolecular) interactions, which are also responsible for the non-ideal behavior of real gases.

Chemisorption is a type of adsorption whereby a molecule adheres to a surface through the formation of a chemical bond, as opposed to the Van der Waals forces which cause physisorption.

Adsorption is usually described through adsorption isotherms, that is, functions which connect the amount of adsorbate on the adsorbent, with its pressure (if gas) or concentration (if liquid).

For liquids (adsorbate) adsorbed on solids (adsorbent), the Langmuir isotherm can be expressed by:

$m = A_{max}\, kc / 1+kc$ [mol g^{-1}, resp. mol.kg^{-1}]

Where:

m - The substance amount of adsorbate adsorbed per gram (or kg) of the adsorbent, the unit is mol g^{-1}, resp. mol.kg^{-1}

A_{max} - the maximal substance amount of adsorbate per gram (or kg) of the adsorbent, the unit is mol g^{-1}, resp. mol.kg^{-1}

k - The adsorption constant (mol^{-1} dm^3)

c - The concentration of adsorbate in liquid (mol dm^{-3})

Apparatus required:

Boiling flasks

Erlenmeyer's flasks

Funnels

Burettes

Titrimetric flasks

Pipettes,

Holders for funnel,

Holders for burettes,

Filtering paper,

Wessel for weighing coal,

Rubber stoppers,

Material required:

Solution of acetic acid

Solution of NaOH,

Activated charcoal,

Phenolphthalein.

Procedure:

Prepare aqueous solutions of acetic acid into numbered flasks following the scheme given in the table. The total volume of each solution is 60 ml. Use flasks fitted with stoppers.

Table 1 Scheme for acetic acid dilution

flask No	V(acetic acid)(cm^3)	V(distilled water)(cm^3)
1	6	54
2	12	48
3	18	42
4	30	30
5	42	18
6	60	0

2 Transfer 10 ml of the solution from each flask into numbered titrimetric flask. Final volume of acetic acid solution is VA = 50 ml per flask.

3 Determine the actual concentration of acetic acid in flasks by titration in this way: For titration, modify the volume in each titrimetric flask. Take away defined volume of the solution, to obtain in each flask the volume as given in the Table 2.

Table 2 Volumes of the acetic acid solutions (V) used for titration before and after adsorption

titrimetric flask No.	1	2	3	4	5	6
volume solution - V [ml]	10	10	5	5	5	2

4 Add 1-2 drops of phenolphthalein and titrate by NaOH.

5 Once the endpoint has been reached, read the burette. The volume of the base (X_i^o) - ml that was required to reach the endpoint write down to the Table 3. 6 Calculate the actual concentration of acetic acid before adsorption (C_i^o) in the flask No.1-6, respectively according Equation 2:

$C_i^o = X_i^o C_T / V$ [mol dm^{-3}]

Where,

X_i^o =is the volume of the titrant before adsorption (NaOH)

C_T =is the volume of the titrant (NaOH)

V =is the volume of the analyte

7 Using practical balance and Wessel for weighing coal, weigh 6 portions of activated charcoal, each portion 5 g. The accuracy of weighing must be with accuracy 0.01 g.

8 Put activated charcoal into numbered flasks with stoppers (1 portion per flask).

9 Plug up the flasks, and shake them. Wait for 20 minutes, the process of adsorption is in progress. Mix the mixtures for several times by flasks shaking within this period. Remark: The process of adsorption is a function of time too. It is important to put char- coal into flasks at the same time, to provide adsorption for the same period in each flask.

10 Filter the mixtures into clean and dry flasks. To avoid disturbing effect of adsorption of acetic acid into filtering paper, remove away the first portion of filtration, app. 5 ml.

11 Determine the final concentration of acetic acid (C_i) in each of the flasks after adsorption: From each solution, transfer the asked volume into clean and dry titrimetric flask, again following Table 2.

12 Repeat points 4-6, and from the consumed base (X_i) from Table 3 determine the concentration of acetic acid (C_i) after adsorption according equation:

$C_i = X_i C_T / V$ [mol dm^{-3}]

Where

X_i = the volume of the titrant after adsorption (NaOH)

C_T & V = the same values as in Equation 2

Table 3 Experimental data

flask No	X_i^o(ml)	C_i^o[mol dm^{-3}]	X_i(ml)	C_i [mol dm^{-3}]	m_i [m mol g^{-1}]	1/ C_i [dm3 mol-1]	1/mi [g mmol-1]

Data treatment

Determination of the substance amount of acetic acid adsorbed per gram of the charcoal mi (m mol g^{-1}) in individual flask:

$m_i = (C_i^o - C_i)V_A/g$

Where,

C_i^o= concentration of acetic acid before adsorption

C_i = concentration of acetic acid after adsorption

V_A= volume of the liquid phase used for adsorption

g = the mass of the adsorbent – charcoal

i= 1-6 the number of flask

Determination of k and Amax

The Equation 1 one can rearrange into a form:

$1/m_i = 1/A_{max} + 1/k\,A_{max}.C_i$

$1/m_i = f(1/C_i)$ should be a straight line

The slope represents the value of $1/k\,A_{max}$

Intercept corresponds to $1/A_{max}$

Result:

$1/k\,A_{max}$ =

$1/A_{max}$ =

Experiment no -24

Saponification/acid value of an oil

Theory of experiment: Saponification is the process by which the fatty acids in the glycerides of the oil are hydrolyzed by an alkali. The resultant salts of fatty acids are called soaps. Saponification value is the amount (mg) of alkali required to saponify a definite quantity (1g) of an oil or fat.

$C_3H_5\ (C_{17}H_{35}COO)_3 + 3KOH = C_3H_5(OH)_3 + 3C_{17}H_{35}\cdot COOK$

Stearin Glycerol Potassium stearate

A known amount of fat or oil is refluxed with an excess amount of alcoholic KOH. After saponification, the amount of KOH is estimated by titrating against standard acid. This will give the amount of KOH utilized for saponification.

Apparatus required:

Conical flask
Few pieces of pumice
Burette
Pipette
Reflux condenser

Materials required:

0.5N HCl
0.5N alcoholic KOH solution
1% phenolphthalein indicator

Procedure:

•Melt the sample if it is not already liquid and filter through paper to remove any impurities and traces of moisture. The sample must be completely moisture-free.

• Accurately weigh 2-5g of oil in 250ml conical flask.

• Add 25-50ml of alcoholic KOH from burette to dissolve the fat completely.

• Prepare a blank also by taking only alcoholic KOH same quantity used in the sample and allowing it to drain at the same duration of time.

• Attach the reflux condenser with the flask.

• Reflux the content by gentle boiling in a water bath for 1 hour. • Cool the flask to room temperature.

• Add few drops of phenolphthalein indicator.

• Titrate the content with 0.5N HCl.

Observation:

S. No	Weight of Sample (g)	Blank titre value (b)	Sample titre value (a)
1			
2			
3			

Calculation:

Saponification Value of oil (S.V.) = (b-a) x 28.05 / Wt. of sample (g)

1ml of 0.5N HCl = 28.06 mg KOH

Result:
Saponification value =

Precaution:
i)Please ensure that all glassware like is Pipette, Burette, Conical flask etc. are clean and free of any impurities.
ii) Carry out the titration most accurately.

Experiment no-25

Aim:

1. To verify the Beer–Lambert's Law using a spectrophotometer.
2. To determine the concentration of an unknown solution from its absorbance.

Theory of experiment: Beer–Lambert's Law states:

$$A = \varepsilon c l$$

Where:

A = Absorbance (unitless)
ε = Molar absorptivity ($L \cdot mol^{-1} \cdot cm^{-1}$)
c = Concentration of the solution ($mol \cdot L^{-1}$)
l = Path length of the cuvette (cm)

According to the law:

Absorbance is directly proportional to concentration for a given wavelength.
Transmittance (T) is related to absorbance as:

$$A = -\log_{10} T$$

$T = I/I_0$ x fraction of light transmitted

By preparing a series of standard solutions and measuring their absorbance at the wavelength of maximum absorbance (λmax), we can plot A vs. C and check for linearity. The slope gives **ε**.
Once the calibration curve is established, the concentration of an unknown can be found by interpolating from the graph.

Apparatus and Materials required:

Spectrophotometer (UV-Vis or colorimeter)
Matched quartz or glass cuvettes (1 cm path length)
Pipettes and micropipettes
Volumetric flasks (10, 25, 50, 100 mL)
Beakers
Distilled water
Standard stock solution of the solute (e.g., potassium dichromate, copper sulfate, or dye solution)
Unknown solution (same solute type)
Tissue paper (lint-free) for wiping cuvettes

Procedure:

A. Determination of λmax

1. Prepare a test solution of intermediate concentration from the stock.
2. Switch on the spectrophotometer and allow it to warm up (\~10 min).
3. Select the wavelength scanning mode.
4. Fill a clean cuvette with distilled water (blank) and place it in the reference holder. Zero the instrument.
5. Measure absorbance of the test solution over a suitable wavelength range (e.g., 350–700 nm).
6. Record the wavelength at which absorbance is maximum (λmax).

B. Verification of Beer–Lambert's Law

1. Prepare a series of standard solutions from the stock solution with known concentrations (e.g., 0.1 M, 0.08 M, 0.06 M, 0.04 M, 0. 02 M).
2. Set the spectrophotometer at λmax determined above.
3. Zero the instrument with distilled water.
4. Measure and record the absorbance of each standard solution.
5. Plot a graph of Absorbance (y-axis) vs. Concentration (x-axis).
6. Check for linearity – a straight line through the origin confirms Beer–Lambert's law.

C. Determination of Concentration of Unknown solution:

1. Measure the absorbance of the unknown solution at λmax.
2. Using the calibration curve, find the corresponding concentration.

Observations:

A.Determination of λmax

S.N.	Wavelength (nm)	Absorbance (A)
1		
2		
3		

λmax = ……. nm

B. Verification of Beer–Lambert's Law

S.N	Concentration ($mol \cdot L^{-1}$)	Absorbance (A)

C. Unknown Sample:

Absorbance of unknown = ...
Concentration from calibration curve = ... $mol \cdot L^{-1}$

Calculations:

From Beer–Lambert's Law:

ε = slope of A vs. C / l

(For l = 1 cm, slope $\approx \varepsilon$)

For unknown sample:
Use slope from calibration curve:

$c_{unknown} = A_{unknown} / \varepsilon .l$

Result

λmax of the given solution = ...nm
Molar absorptivity (ε) = ...$L \cdot mol^{-1} \cdot cm^{-1}$
Concentration of unknown solution = ...$mol \cdot L^{-1}$

Precautions

1. Use clean, dry cuvettes and handle only by the frosted sides.
2. Avoid bubbles or fingerprints on cuvettes.
3. Always zero the instrument with the blank solution.
4. Use freshly prepared solutions to avoid degradation.
5. Ensure the spectrophotometer is warmed up before measurements.

Experiment no-26

Aim: Determination of the Calorific Value of Fuels Using a Bomb Calorimeter

Theory of experiment: The calorific value of a fuel is the total amount of heat released when a unit mass (solid/liquid) or unit volume (gas) of the fuel undergoes complete combustion under standard conditions.
It is usually expressed in kJ/kg (for solids and liquids) or kJ/m³ (for gases).

A bomb calorimeter is an instrument designed to measure this heat of combustion. The fuel sample is burned in an oxygen-rich environment inside a strong steel bomb, which is immersed in a known quantity of water. The heat released during combustion is absorbed by the surrounding water and the calorimeter body, causing a measurable temperature rise.

The Higher Calorific Value (HCV) includes the latent heat of vaporization of water formed during combustion, while the Lower Calorific Value (LCV) excludes it.

Formula for HCV:

$$HCV = (W + w) \times \Delta T - e_1 / m$$

Where:

W = Mass of water in the calorimeter (kg)
w = Water equivalent of calorimeter (kg)
ΔT = Rise in temperature (°C)
e_1 = Correction for fuse wire, cotton thread, etc. (kJ)
m = Mass of fuel sample (kg)

Formula for LCV:

$$LCV = HCV - \{(9 \times H \times 2.26) / (100)\}$$

Where:
H = Percentage of hydrogen in fuel
2.26 = Latent heat of vaporization of water (MJ/kg)

Apparatus and Materials required:

Bomb calorimeter assembly (including steel bomb, water jacket, thermometer, and stirrer)
Oxygen cylinder with regulator
Ignition system (fuse wire and cotton thread)
Weighing balance (accuracy ±0.1 mg)
Distilled water
Sample of fuel (e.g., coal, kerosene, diesel, biomass)
Calorimeter accessories (pressure gauge, sealing rings, etc.)

Procedure:

Preparation

1. Clean and dry the bomb and crucible thoroughly.
2. Weigh accurately about 0.8–1.0 g of the fuel sample using the analytical balance.
3. Place the fuel sample in the crucible.
4. Attach a measured length of fuse wire across the electrodes, ensuring that it touches the sample.
5. Place a small cotton thread to assist ignition if necessary.

B. Charging the Bomb

6. Fit the cover tightly and charge the bomb with oxygen to about 25–30 atm pressure using the oxygen cylinder.
7. Place the bomb inside the calorimeter bucket containing a known quantity of water W.
8. Note the initial water temperature.

C. Combustion

9. Insert the thermometer and stirrer into the calorimeter.
10. Connect the fuse wire to the ignition terminals.
11. Start gentle stirring and allow the temperature to stabilize.
12. Ignite the sample electrically; record the maximum temperature attained.

D. Cooling

13. Continue stirring until the temperature starts to fall.
14. Remove the bomb, release pressure slowly, and wash the bomb interior.
15. Measure the unburned length of fuse wire to calculate correction for fuse wire combustion.

Observations Table:

Parameter	Symbol	Value	Unit
Mass of fuel sample	m		g
Mass of water in calorimeter	W		Kg
Water equivalent of calorimeter	w		Kg
Initial temperature	T_1		°C
Final temperature	T_2		°C
Rise in temperature	$\Delta T = T_2 - T_1$		°C
Fuse wire correction	e_1		kJ
Hydrogen content of fuel	H		%

Calculations:

1. Calculate HCV using:

$$HCV = (W + w) \times \Delta T - e_1 / m$$

2. Calculate LCV using:

$$LCV = HCV - \{(9 \times H \times 2.26) / (100)\}$$

Precautions:

Ensure the bomb is completely airtight before combustion.
Avoid overcharging the bomb with oxygen to prevent accidents.
Handle oxygen cylinder with care and follow all safety protocols.
Stir the water uniformly to prevent uneven temperature distribution.
Use distilled water to avoid impurities affecting heat absorption.

Result:

The Higher Calorific Value (HCV) of the given fuel sample = … kJ/kg.
The Lower Calorific Value (LCV) of the given fuel sample = … kJ/kg.

Experiment no-27

Aim:

1. To study the physical and chemical properties of ion exchange resins.
2. To determine the ion exchange capacity of a given resin sample.

Theory of experiment:

Ion exchange resins are insoluble, high-molecular-weight polymers containing ionizable functional groups. They can exchange specific ions within a solution without altering the polymer's structure. Depending on the functional groups, they are classified as cation exchangers (replace positive ions) or anion exchangers (replace negative ions).

When a resin comes in contact with an electrolyte solution, ions from the resin are exchanged with ions of similar charge from the solution. The efficiency of a resin is expressed in terms of its ion exchange capacity, which is the number of milli-equivalents of ions exchanged per gram of dry resin.

In a cation exchange resin, hydrogen ions (H^+) are exchanged for cations (e.g., Na^+, Ca^{2+}) from the solution. In an anion exchange resin, hydroxide ions (OH^-) are exchanged for anions (e.g., Cl^-, SO_4^{2-}). The general reaction for a cation exchanger in hydrogen form is:

$$R\text{-}H + Na^+ \rightarrow R\text{-}Na + H^+$$

Where:

R= resin matrix
H = hydrogen ion bound to resin
Na^+ = cation from the solution

The ion exchange capacity is calculated as:

Capacity (meq/g) = Volume of titrant (mL) × Normality of titrant / Mass of dry resin (g)

Apparatus and Materials Required:

Ion exchange resin (cation or anion type)
Glass column or burette (50 mL)
Funnel and stand
Conical flask (250 mL)
Beakers (100 mL)
Measuring cylinder (100 mL)
Filter paper and funnel
Stopcock or pinch clip
Distilled water
Standard acid/base solution (e.g., 0.1 N HCl or NaOH)
Indicator (phenolphthalein or methyl orange)
pH meter (optional)

Chemical Reagents required:

Sodium chloride (NaCl) solution (0.1 M) – for regeneration
Standard sodium hydroxide (NaOH) or hydrochloric acid (HCl) solution (0.1 N) – for titration
Distilled water.

Procedure:

A. Preparation of the Resin Column:

1. Weigh about 5 g of dry resin and soak it in distilled water for at least 30 minutes to allow swelling.
2. Prepare a glass column and place a small layer of glass wool at the bottom to prevent resin loss.
3. Pour the swollen resin into the column with the help of a funnel, ensuring no air bubbles are trapped.
4. Wash the resin with distilled water until the effluent is free from fine particles and neutral in pH.

B. Ion Exchange Process:

1. Pass 50 mL of standard NaCl solution (0.1 M) through the resin at a steady flow rate (about 2–3 mL/min).
2. Collect the effluent in a conical flask for analysis.

C. Determination of Exchange Capacity:

1. Take the collected effluent containing H^+ ions (for cation resin) or OH^- ions (for anion resin).
2. Titrate it against standard NaOH (for cation resin) or HCl (for anion resin) using a suitable indicator.
3. Note the volume of titrant used.

D. Regeneration of Resin:

1. Pass 0.1 M NaCl (for anion resin) or 0.1 M HCl (for cation resin) through the column to restore the resin to its original form.
2. Wash thoroughly with distilled water before reuse.

Observations Table:

S. No	Volume of titrant (mL)	Normality of titrant (N)	Mass of dry resin (g)	Ion Exchange Capacity (meq/g)
1				
2				

Calculations:

Ion Exchange Capacity (meq/g) = {Volume of titrant (mL) × Normality of titrant}/{Mass of dry resin (g)}

Results:

The ion exchange capacity of the given resin is found to be: {_____ meq/g}

Precautions:

Ensure the resin is fully swollen before use.
Avoid trapping air bubbles while packing the resin column.
Maintain a steady flow rate to ensure complete ion exchange.
Use freshly prepared standard solutions for accuracy.
Wash the resin properly during regeneration to avoid contamination.

Applications:

Water softening and demineralization
Wastewater treatment
Separation of metal ions in analytical chemistry
Pharmaceutical and food processing industries